This book is a work of fiction. Names, characters, places, and incidents either are products of the author's imagination or are used fictitiously. Any resemblance to actual persons, living or dead, businesses, organizations, events, or locales is entirely coincidental.

Ms. Whit

Written and Illustrated by Debbie Woodward Musselli

Dedication

To the many friends who believed I could do it. I did.

To my daughter Sara, for inspiring me to do it better.
To my cousin Jackie, who planted the seed such a long time ago.
To my sister, Kay who supports this project at every turn.
To my grandson Jeremiah (who is the prince) and finally said yes....you can use my name.
To my grandson Max for being the wind beneath my winglettes.
To my niece, Ronny for believing I could do it....someday.

Someday, is now.

I love you all. Believe it!

Foreword

Oh, Sweet Father Mistletoad! Get ready for a journey along the banks of the West Pearl River in Slidell, Louisiana. Deb has filled this imaginative tale with creatures you've never heard of or imagined. There are so many characters that will warm your heart and make you smile.

Ms Whit's adventures will take you from her home in the older than ancient piano stool to Flatter Rock, from the dreaded hurricane to the Coming Up Celebration. And through it all runs one message…believe in yourself, "see it into being, practice, practice, practice."

This is something Deb has done. She conceived this story many years ago, and never let it go. She believed in it and the joy it could bring to children, young and old. So, she treasured this story in her heart and now has brought it to fruition. Her whimsical illustrations compliments and completes her mission and vision:

Just believe!

I can't wait to share this wonderful story, and the fun Deb brings to life through Ms Whit's Adventures.

Kayla J.W. Marnach
Author of Can-Do Kids Series

Introduction

Have you ever heard music under water, have you listened to the trilling of frogs at night?
Did you ever feel something whiz past your face but never saw anything?
Have you ever met a creature so darling you just wanted to pick it up and hold it all day?

Oh, I have.

Have you ever wondered what it would feel like to fly? Maybe just wish it and it would be….or simply believe it into being. You can, you know. All you have to do is practice. A lot.

That is what Ms. Whit did. Every day. When she raced the HummingBunny, when she dove into the river and listened to the Mussels sing…Oh yes, mussells sing beautifully. When she met the axolotls and…oh no, no, no. If you want to know how that story ends you will have to read on.

Prologue

A long time ago, though I'm not sure how long, Ms. Whit came to live in Slidell by way of New Orleans. New Orleans is in the state of Louisiana. It is a noisy, bustling city that Ms. Whit believed she would not miss if ever she would just pick up and leave it for the wide-open spaces of nothing in the world but peaceful quiet. There could be no finer state to live in, she was sure of it...no better place to be, she was certain; all she ever needed was peaceful quiet. No honking horns, no screaming tires, no smoking exhaust pipes, no smelly garbage trucks, no yelling vendors, no screeching children or barking dogs. She imagined the tranquil countryside and knew she must have it. She could almost taste the clean air. She could live the simple life and not have to dodge the feet of the harried citizens of the great metropolis of New Orleans. She had imagined the tranquility of this peaceful quiet for years. Ms. Whit decided. She packed her traveling bag, told all her friends she was leaving, waved goodbye to Mama and Papa and hopped on back of Lindy Bell's older than ancient faded red, 1954 Ford pickup truck tucked in a box of chilled lettuce heads. This was it. She was off to find her own little corner of paradise.

That was three summers ago.

Now, the way Ms. Whit wound up on Auntie Lo and Uncle Jackwere's great back porch was the first of many adventures. She learned that traveling in the back of a produce truck was not at all peaceful and far from quiet. That first lesson was hard to learn. There were so many things you had to consider. There didn't seem to be anything instant about wanting to reach your destination. Seemed that no matter what it was in life you wanted you had to work for it or you had to practice...a lot.

Ms Whit sighed. She stepped over to the rail of the porch fence, remembering that trip of long ago. How she had come across the great back porch, her beloved piano stool, Auntie Lo, Uncle Jackwere, and Saysa Sweet Peaches, the cat called Chat, Tutankhamen, That Big Old BullFrog Travis, and everything else that made up the search for peaceful quiet Ms. Whit looked for in The Great Backyard that faced the banks of the West Pearl River, which ran through the parish that was the heart of Ms. Whit and Auntie Lo and Uncle Jackwere.

To Ms.Whit the greatest thing in all the world would be to have a little peaceful quiet. It just so happens that finding it is a whole lot different than having it.

First you have to go on a bazillion adventures just to find the right spot and even more importantly, you must be willing, absolutely committed to using your imagination. For just as you think you have it, it suddenly disappears. It being that ever-elusive state of mind, yes, peaceful quiet.

During her journey Ms. Whit came to understand that moving from the city to the country was a tradeoff. Frog songs to some may be a raucous sound, to Ms.Whit it is beautiful music. To some the hustle and bustle of city life is exciting and adventurous, to Ms.Whit it is annoying and bothersome.

She would rather watch the stars or dive into the river off her back porch. Some never go outside, content to be indoors plucking life from virtual streams and tasting bits of canned stew. Some never know the freedom of living out what they imagine. She does. But she didn't always know it. She had to learn. She had to learn how to use her Imagination. She had to learn that thoughts are things.

Ms. Whit is just like you, she loves playing with dragonflies and dancing on lily pads. She adores playing chase with Saysa Sweet Peaches and listening to the old bullfrog crooning to the river. And honestly, the day isn't done until she's singing lullabies to the baby frogs swimming in the "waiting pools," growing big enough to come out of TheWater and live on the banks of the river.

Really, Ms. Whit loves to... hunh.... what? Who is Ms. Whit? Well now, I thought you would never ask! Ms. Whit is a tiny, itsy-bitsy, teeny-weeny, itty-bitty, highly intelligent and most beautiful frog! But please, you must never, ever think she is just a silly old frog or think for one minute she is usual or common. Indeed, she is the most unusual and uncommon frog you will ever know.

So, listen up ya'll...unpack your imagination and let me tell you just one of the stories about Ms. Whit's adventures with her unusual friends on her uncommon search for that ever-elusive state of peaceful quiet. Does it exist? Is there such a place in all the world? Let us find out.

Table of Contents

Deb Musselli 2015

Chapter One

Ms. Whit

Ms. Whit lives in an older than ancient piano stool. Down the center of the stool is a long, narrow hole where a long, threaded bar used to fit. You could turn the seat up or down as you needed to fit under the keyboard to play the piano. It was the sort of seat you could spin around and around on until you'd get a wee bit dizzy and maybe your Mama would tell you to 'stop that spinning'. If you have ever sat on one, you know the kind I'm talking about. To get inside she must scoot backwards down the hole for there is little room to turn around. Her house sits beside the porch swing snuggled up close to the rail of the porch.

It is from this very spot that most all Ms. Whit's adventures begin. Early every morning, before it is light out, she scoots out of the hole and jumps down to the floor, she hops over the walkway and across the yard to the wooden deck of the boat dock Uncle Jackwere built. She sits on the edge of the dock in the shadow of a two by four facing the West Pearl River, waiting for the sun to rise. When it does, she will dive to the bottom of the river. Have you ever been to a river bottom? I can tell you it is a very unique experience if you are this frog.

When Ms. Whit dives into the river 'things' begin to happen. Not regular things...not the things that would happen to you or to me. The things that happen to her are mostly uncommon and highly unusual. Some would say those things may be highly unlikely, but I do not agree. I saw what I saw, and I heard what I heard.

Ms. Whit sat, humming for anyone who might be listening, facing the river knowing that when she opened her eyes the sun would have risen, glittering and sparkling like magical diamonds strewn across TheWater.

It was this very moment she waited for, as where the sun sparkled brightest, Ms. Whit dove into the river. She dove into the exact same spot every morning because she knew who would be at the bottom of the river.

The mussels would be there. Mussels are creatures who look very much like clams. Course they aren't. and you will not find a pearl in a mussel.

Mussels can't walk ...'cause they have no legs. Mussels don't really swim; they don't have any arms. Mussels don't do much of anything, but when they do, they sing. Oh how mussels love to sing. They sing underwater songs mostly. That is what they know about.

If they could, they would sing all the time and never stop singing. They would rather sing than eat, which is the only other thing mussels love to do.

Unfortunately, they do stop singing. Every time a shadow moves across TheWater or if a Human gets too close, they just stop.

You see, mussels are very, very, very shy when it comes to singing. That is why nobody ever heard a mussel sing before. Except Ms. Whit. She dives to the river bottom every morning just to hear the mussels sing... and they will sing about anything.

They sing about the flow of the river and the warmth of sunbeams, muddy rocks and duckweed, moon-glades and crawdads, fireworks and shooting stars, boat motors and drifting wood, dangling feet and the fisherman's lure, fireflies and stormy skies, clouds, kites, duck bottoms, skimming rocks and wooden docks, currents and UFOs...Unidentified Floating Objects, magpies, dragonflies, fish of all sorts and boysenberry pies...boysenberry pies?

No! Mussels have never had a song about a boysenberry pie...my stars, whoever heard of such a thing! By the way, what is a boysenberry anyway? Well, mussels sing about almost anything. So, this morning, when Ms. Whit dove into the river, at the precise time the sun sparkled on TheWater, she dove straight to the little pod of mussels singing a cappella on the silty bottom of the West Pearl River.

Now listen y'all, you must understand the delicate nature of getting close enough to the mussels to hear them sing. Ms. Whit has to be so careful when she dives into the river, for just the slightest motion the mussels are not sure of will make them clam up tight and it could be many hours before they get over their fright and shyness and be willing to venture out of their shells to sing again.

So, very carefully and oh so gingerly, Ms. Whit alights on the long dead tree stump to listen to the mussels sing.

The Song of the Mussels cannot be described in words that you or I could understand. But I can tell you that when they sing, the whole entire river comes alive with music. The sleepy underwater inhabitants wake to the melodies of these uncommonly beautiful and unusually shy creatures.

Ms. Whit adores spending time with the mussels when they are singing. But it is a quick visit. She can only stay for a little while. So, every morning she tries to sit and listen without disturbing the underwater choir. She grabs hold of the stump with her long slender toes trying desperately hard to keep perfectly still. The current is strong and tries to carry her away, but she holds on tight and listens to the beautiful harmonies.

Oh, how glorious the sounds! Everywhere there is music. Of course, being underwater you feel the music. Just as it is when two stones are struck together underwater, one can feel the sound. Now imagine music underwater, you can feel it too. You can feel the rhythm. You can feel the beat, the tempo and the sheer joy of every note. Imagine! Ms. Whit imagines. And that is precisely why she cannot be still.

The music from the mussels courses through her entire body as the sound waves lift her from the watery perch. She closes her eyes and sways left, the volume rises and Ms. Whit sways right. As she is caught up in the whimsical strain of the liquid melody, Ms. Whit's foot begins to tap...her fingers start to strum a silent beat against the waterlogged wood of the hollow old tree stump. She lets go of the wood and rises softly, turning and twirling to the rhythm of the wonderful sounds. She swims fast and slow, high and low, spiraling and spinning around and around. She passes the sleepy blue gill, soars by the curious crawdads and dances past the many creatures living on the river's muddy floor.

Deb Musselli 2015

Oh, to be this frog! Ms. Whit never tires of the music the mussels make...which is the very reason she waits for the sun to rise and sparkle on the river.

The song was over. Now she must hurry. She must reach the surface of TheWater before she runs out of air. She waved goodbye to her friends then pushed hard against the stump springing toward the surface. Hurry! Hurry! Oh! Great Father MistleToad! Why had she waited so long? Her cheeks were straining, and turning pale blue as she burst through the surface gasping for air. A-a-aaaahhhhh!" she spurted loudly...for a frog. "Silly frog, silly thing you," she scolded herself., "Why, you could have drowned, can you imagine what they'd say...can't you hear it now," The Frog Drowns"...that would be the headlines...frogs seldom drown...think about it, most unfortunate...have to use the bottom time more carefully, any diver knows that.... but those songs! Has anyone ever heard them...oh, the world would be blessed if the world could hear one song. She swam to the lily pad nearest her and hopped onto the wide circular leaf. Leaning into a shadow she jumped into the pale pink blossom. She sank into a soft cool petal and closed her eyes to rest for just a moment. She could hear the drone far in the distance. She was getting sleepy. Her eyes were heavy. There was peace and quiet at....

"LAWN MOWER! LAWN MOWER!" the dragonfly screamed shrilly.

Ms. Whit sprang from the lily pad when Dolly buzzed overhead, warning the entire river of the impending doom! It must be Tuesday she mumbled, her heart racing from the sudden start. The frogs hopped behind the rocks. The crickets jumped under the house. The bees droned away, they didn't care. The June bugs snuggled into the dirt. The ants were too low to worry. The lawn mower couldn't catch them so close to the ground.

The worms turned over in their snuggly beds. Lizards ran up the wall. Squirrels took to the trees and birds followed behind the mower picking up the delicious morsels the lawn mower so thoughtfully uncovered.

"You better take shelter! You better run! You better fly fast! Rocks and rubble stones and grass, bottle caps, sticks and bright pretty glass! It flies like a rocket and pings off the wall. Hurry up everyone! Time to get clear! It's the very first Tuesday and mowin' day's here! Lawn mower! Lawn mower!" screamed Dolly with every ounce of yelling she could muster.

Dolly was the herald each time the mower came out of the shed. It was brought out every Tuesday, but Dolly didn't know the difference between a month and a week. Ms. Whit watched the dragonfly soar through the air as Uncle Jackwere went about his weekly routine.

Sufficiently recovered now, Ms. Whit sat on the lily pad watching for her friend. She knew it wouldn't be long before Saysa Sweet Peaches arrived for their morning race. That creature was an enigma to the Frog. Saysa Sweet Peaches is a HummingBunny. HummingBunnies are very rare and very, very, very fast. If you have never seen one, that is probably the reason. Unlike Ms. Whit's underwater friends the mussels, HummingBunnies don't sing. They hum. That is how they communicate with each other and the few friends they are able to make.

HummingBunnies believe it is because they are so fast...or maybe other creatures are simply too slow. However it works out, the little creatures pretty much stick together being the birds of fur and feather that they are. Of course, if you really want to see a HummingBunny you will have to use your imagination. You do practice using your imagination don't you? Sure, you do! You have to practice every day to get good at it. Practice, practice, practice, again and again. Ms. Whit's mother, Delilah told her those words every day when she was growing up. If Mama said it was so, it must be. So, Ms. Whit practiced using her imagination every single day.

As a matter of fact, Ms. Whit was practicing using her imagination on the first day she met Saysa Sweet Peaches. It has been some time ago, though I can't remember how long Ms. Whit was sitting on the handrail imagining what it would be like to get to Flatter Rock from The Great Back Porch. Of course, in the usual scheme of things it isn't difficult at all. You swim down the river or hop along the bank. Both are good ways, though swimming upstream on the way back home can wear you out. However, on the day the two met, Ms. Whit wasn't imagining how to swim or hop down the river to Flatter Rock.

She was imagining how it would feel if she could fly. Now, we all know that frogs don't fly. Just the same, Ms. Whit was practicing on what it would feel like if she were flying. She was deep in thought, concentrating, imagining, seeing herself soaring through the air flapping her arms as fast as they would go... it was hard work flying, birds made it look so easy. She tried to see it clearly, to be flight. Thoughts are things, thoughts are things. She decided she needed a new approach. Maybe, if she were to jump out into space and spin her arms in circles she could get the momentum going and take off into the air. That's it. She could try that. As she leaned forward to begin the launch, she felt an amazingly fast buzz rush past her ear. Then she heard a rapid whirring sound unlike anything she had ever heard. It sounded like brrrrrrrr-eeeeeeeet! She blinked her eyes, maybe she had imagined the sound. She was imagining flying so maybe all sorts of odd things happened when you begin to use your Imagination. She closed her eyes, preparing to launch again. Arms out...lean forward.....brrrrrrrr-eeeeeeeet! Opening her eyes she saw a flash of movement. A bee rose from one of the huge late blooming morning glories...she knew it wasn't the bee. She closed her eyes and imagined the air beneath her lift her from the tip of a cattail bloom, again the odd whirring sound. Ms. Whit opened her eyes. The sound was following the movement, she saw the thing speeding through the air then heard the sound. She stood motionless, straining her bright eyes, focusing all her attention on the erratically moving morning glory. She stared intently at the exact spot she'd last seen movement. Not moving her eyes off the focal point, she began hopping towards the blossom. What was that thing? She climbed over a curling tendril from the flower's vine and watched as the shape of the oddest-looking creature she had ever witnessed on The Great Back Porch began to take form. The vibration slowed and the creature flew inside the pollen drenched flower alighting on the soft petals. Ms. Whit had not yet learned to fly so she hopped and climbed over the leaves to the mouth of the flower. There it was, it was beautiful! But what was it? It swam in the pollen as if the flower were a tub. It was bathing in the nectar of the flower. Pollen flew about, covering everything in its path with golden, sweet powder. Ms. Whit stood on tiptoe while the gold dust settled on her small little form covering her from hat to toe.

She looked into the face of a small...er...well...a bunny, humming. It was furry like a bunny and feathered like a bird. It was beautiful. The most extraordinary creature she could ever remember seeing. Its wings shimmered in the sunshine filtering through the flower petals. The iridescent colors blended in and out with the color of its fur that covered all but its wings. The ears were streamlined, made for flight, the nose of the bunny...no, bird...does a bird have a nose, this one did. Its nose was a tiny button at the bottom of a proboscis it used for gathering nectar from all the millions of flowers growing in The Great Backyard. No wonder Auntie Lo's gardens were always so beautifully dressed. It was a hummingbird and it was a bunny. The little thing sat up in the morning glory and looked straight at Ms. Whit. It grinned the biggest grin Ms. Whit had ever seen on a face so small. Then the creature began to hum.

Not a slow hum. Not the kind of hum we would hum. Not a Mother's-in-the-kitchen-baking-cookies hum. This was a sonic hum. A hum so fast it was a sound blur. Ms. Whit was amazed. She stared at the creature in utter fascination. She didn't mean to be rude, but she couldn't help but stare, her eyes were riveted on the creature's face. The humming bunny leaned closer to the frog's face and hummed so fast it was no more than a buzz. Ms. Whit did not have a clue, not even an inkling of an idea what the little bunny...or bird...bunnybird? No, she was clearly a humming bunny... with wings...she did not know what the creature wanted from her.

What was it saying? What did it want? Where did it come from? Ms. Whit didn't know what to do. The creature wanted something. It was happy to be there in the flower, happy to be humming, happy Ms. Whit was there it seemed. But what was it telling her? Couldn't she or he see the confusion all over Ms. Whit's face? Clearly, there was a communication problem. Ms. Whit sat and listened and watched; nodding and smiling as if she could really understand exactly what the little creature who was swiftly gesturing and flitting hither, thither and yon was talking about. Ms. Whit was getting dizzy. How long could it go on this way?

To Ms. Whit's great and utter relief, the little humming bunny stopped humming. Slowly, almost meticulously the creature hummed. "Hello, my friend," she said joyfully. "My name is Saysa Sweet Peaches...I am a HummingBunny, who are you? What is your name? How did you come to see me? Nobody sees me when I come to this place." Saysa Sweet Peaches said.

"Well, glory is the day! You do talk!" Ms. Whit was pleased. "I am a frog...I am called Ms. Whit, I was practicing...that is how I came to see you. I was practicing on how it would feel if I could fly." Ms. Whit ended a little sheepishly.

"Flying is the best fun ever. I fly everywhere I go, unless I see it into being." Saysa stated.

"Unless you do what?' Ms. Whit asked curiously.

See it into being? Thoughts are things! Ms. Whit's mind was racing. What did this funny little creature know?

"See it into being, you know, when you imagine something so thoroughly, see every detail in vivid color and sound and smell that it… just is." Saysa concluded.

DMasselli

"Sure, I... I know exactly what you mean, I think." Ms Whit said. What was it she said? See it into being? Thoughts are things! There was something about to happen to Ms. Whit. She could feel it in her bones. This HummingBunny was going to play a major role in Ms. Whit's future.

Saysa talked to Ms. Whit for a good long while, she told her she lived in the top of the tallest pine tree in a nest built of cattail down and tender grapevines. She told her the history of HummingBunnies and how they lived from east to west and places far beyond. They race the wind; they eat nectar and are very clever creatures. They make the best of friends, if ever you can find one.

Even now to this very day, Ms. Whit was still amazed at the little creature she'd met so long ago. From that first day, Saysa Sweet Peaches has been teacher and friend. She understands the way things work that not many creatures get. She knew "things". Mostly unusual and uncommon things. Saysa Sweet Peaches had known there was something she could teach Ms. Whit. She'd known it the moment she saw her. She'd known they would be best friends. She understood it would take time for her friend to accept some of the things that were right under her nose. It would take time and practice for her to believe. Practice. Practice. Practice. That is what Saysa Sweet Peaches' mother taught her from a very early age.

Today was the day of a special race. Ms. Whit had charted a course unlike any of the others she'd done before. She had a notion that today was going to be different.

"Good morning my friend, I hope you are ready for this. I have created a route so intricate you cannot possibly get through it all before I reach the last lily pad. Today is the day...I can feel it. I can feel the win, I can see the end of the race and I am the victor!" Ms. Whit was positive she would be victorious. The HummingBunny chuckled a humming response and lit beside Ms. Whit, her wings folding gently behind her. She licked the nectar off her paws and scratched behind her ear. She waited for instructions as she did practically every morning. This was the practice she devised for Ms. Whit to prepare her for the time when she could reveal the secret all HummingBunnies have always known. It wouldn't be long, she surmised; the little frog was nearly ready.

The two sat side by side on the edge of the dock as Ms. Whit laid out the course. They were to start at the dock, Ms. Whit's course would be to reach the last lily pad on the right side of the river. It was not a long course compared to the flying ace. She would hop, swim, jump and practically fly from the dock to the lily pad at the end of the course. For the HummingBunny the route was designed to match her skills. Her skill at speed was unmatched by any living creature in the parish. No one could beat her. Ms. Whit laid out the route. Fly to the roof of Auntie Toa's house, knock three times on the roof, follow the river to Down Below where the Old Bullfrog sleeps under the shade of the elephant ears, grab the pebble from beneath the ledge of Flatter Rock, cross over to the pond, up the walkway, over the stone mushroom, through the front yard to the bird house on the bending pine, then to the stack of cheese boxes outside the kitchen window, tap the window twice, then up to the roof and down the chimney, out the window over the lilac bush, pass the butterfly house and Lord Chatterly's scratching post, say hello to Boxie and meet me at the lily pad at the end of my course. She looked into the eyes of the HummingBunny. They exchanged an understanding of what was expected one from the other. A fair race and good form. Ms. Whit grinned wide. They raced almost every morning and so far, the outcome was always the same. Not winning the race didn't seem to faze Ms. Whit. She really tried to beat the little blur of a creature, but not once did she come even close to reaching the last lily pad before the HummingBunny got there. She never complained and never made excuses. She gave it her all every single time. Ms. Whit simply would not give up. Racing the HummingBunny was much the same as racing the wind or trying to catch a falling star. She knew she wasn't really competing with Saysa Sweet Peaches. She knew she never had been. She was competing with her own best effort. Racing herself. Trying every day to beat her best. And every day she did just that.

Saysa Sweet Peaches grinned as wide as Ms. Whit. In all the races they had run, all the cockamamie, harebrained, farfetched crazy places Ms. Whit had the HummingBunny run off to, Ms. Whit never tired of getting one lily pad closer to winning. Even the HummingBunny knew that for her friend, it wasn't about winning the race against unbeatable odds. It was about beating her best time, getting better, getting stronger. Learning to see the prize. Most importantly, it was using her Imagination to the fullest.

Ms. Whit's voice echoed across the river bank up and down as she shouted. "On your toes! Get ready, Bunnybird! I'm coming for you! On to victory!" She leaned into the breeze. "Go! Go! Go!"

Ms. Whit dove into the water. Swimming faster than she had ever done before. She jumped onto the first lily pad...quickly she hopped across the wide leaf onto the second lily pad, then to the third one. Her heart was racing wildly as she skimmed the fourth one. She hopped across the water to the fifth lily pad, slipping across the slick surface on to the sixth one. Hurrying ever faster, she leaped onto the seventh lily pad. Above her head she felt the whoosh of the HummingBunny followed by the inevitable sound, brrrrrrrr-eeeeeeeet! Ms. Whit knew she had only fractions of a second to reach the last lily pad. She leaned into the last jump and with all her might dove for the last bobbing leaf.

Their shoulders touched. Together they hit the leaf in an explosion of water and celebration. She did it. It was the first time she'd come this close to winning. Oh, this was it...the sheer joy of achievement. Ms. Whit and Saysa Sweet Peaches jumped about the lily pad, flipping, twisting and shouting in pure happiness. It was one of those rare moments of perfection. They would have many more times to share these incredible discoveries as Ms. Whit came to recognize what believing in herself was all about. What "Thoughts are things" meant in the whole scheme of things.

A group of tadpoles gathered around the lily pad, listening to Ms. Whit translate Saysa Sweet Peaches' account of things that were happening on the river. The frog smiled as Saysa handed her a sparkling pebble she'd retrieved from under Flatter Rock. As for the happenings around this part of the parish, it was the usual routine. From Auntie Lo's to Down Below, and from Auntie Toadie McRoadie's to Flatter Rock all was quiet along the river up and down...at least for the time being.

Saysa Sweet Peaches bid her friends farewell but before they could say goodbye the HummingBunny was gone. The little frog shook her head at the way Saysa Sweet Peaches made her exits. The HummingBunny didn't fly away, she simply disappeared.

Ms. Whit hopped across the trail of lily pads onto the dock Uncle Jackwere had so thoughtfully built, she met Boxie Tortusie sunning on the dock. Upon Boxie's wide green back rested his three younger brothers.

"Good morning everyone!" Ms. Whit called to them cheerfully.

"Semela ona you, semala ona you. Ama no believe essa such a bela morning," Boxie replied. Boxie answered her the same way every morning no matter if it was sunny, raining, cold, windy or hot. Then the familiar echo of "g'mornin'! g'mornin'! g'mornin'! came from Boxie's younger brothers. Ms. Whit hopped onto the faded wooden planks of the boardwalk and headed for the Great Back Porch.

RoBin
7-1
B-3
Deb Musselli

Chapter Two
Okra Pods

Ms. Whit hopped onto the piano stool. She scooted down the hole and rummaged around for her traveling bag. There were muffled noises coming from Auntie Lo and Uncle Jackwere's house. She was curious about the noise but wasn't paying enough attention to warrant an investigation. She would check in on the Humans later. She was on a mission now. She needed to get to Flatter Rock. There were big things happening on the river today. Big things. Frogs from all over would be gathering for the next Coming Up. It would be an epic celebration. She needed to be there early today so she could practice with Mildred and the new dancing troupe Mildred found, The Frogettes. She hoped they were as good as Mildred said they were. She supposed Mildred would know; Mildred knew music. She played every percussion instrument there was to play. Usually more than one at a time.

Once outside the hole she put the traveling bag over her shoulder. The instant she turned to hop from the stool, there was a loud and thunderous crash from inside the kitchen. The terrible noise startled her so badly she lost her balance and flip-flopping in midair she fell from the stool. Ms. Whit feared the worst. She would probably be squashed when she hit the floor. What a way to go! She shut her eyes and braced herself for the crash.

She felt the soft squish of gooey, slimy, cold wet stuff. Was she dead? She opened her eyes to survey the damage and, to her surprise, discovered she had landed in a large bowl of cut up okra pods. Sticky juice clung from her ever-present hat to her long slender toes.

This was quite enough! Her heart was pounding as she sat in the thick okra goo. She looked around not knowing if the awful noise would come again. She peeked over the bowl. No, no signs of an earthquake. There had not been any earthquakes in Slidell for as long as she knew to remember. Really! What on earth was going on? Holding on to the thin rim of the enamel coated bowl, she slipped over the side onto the floor.

She would find out what all the racket was about, but first, she had to get the sticky off. What a mess. Surely, she had something in her bag, an old rag or a bit of cloth perhaps. Anything to wipe this icky, sticky stuff off. It felt like glue. She opened her traveling bag and began rummaging through the contents. She pulled out a wide assortment of useful things she found handy to have on her travels. A bit of string, a cap from a tiny bottle, the pebble from Saysa Sweet Peaches, a tiny ball of twine, a miniature silver spoon her Mama said she was born with, a bit of mirrored glass, a variety of dried herbs, and one very old and tarnished copper coin. Oh dear, had she no cloth? Nothing to use for removing okra juice? Digging to the bottom of the bag, she felt the cheesecloth. Ah, that's better, cloth. Now she was getting somewhere. She pulled the cloth from the bag and immediately began to wipe at the sticky sweet juice.

"Hurmpf," she mumbled, frustrated as she worked, thinking about wretched okra and not having any peace and quiet. Could the Humans not find anything better to do than scare her half to death.

Ms. Whit had been wiping at the juice with the stringy cheesecloth for some time before she realized it was beginning to stick to her skin. Wiping at her face, the cloth stuck to her hands. Using her feet, she got the cloth off her hands, but now it was stuck to her feet. She tried pulling it off her feet and wound up with it stuck to both hands and feet! Sweet Mistle Toad. Would this stuff never come off her fingers! For several minutes, she wrestled with the cheesecloth trying desperately to get out of its gluey grip. This wasn't working.

The harder she fought its hold, the tighter it wrapped around her. Finally, she had to give up. She was stuck. She sat for a minute, peeking through a small slit in the cloth.

What an utterly ridiculous sight she was. She looked like a tiny mummy. Her entire body was wrapped in cheesecloth from her head to the tops of her feet. Even her hat was stuck to her head. Ms. Whit lay on the floor. Her body was rigid. But her belly began to shake, her cheeks brushed against the stiff cloth. It had become scratchy and dried out. Ms. Whit began to laugh. She couldn't help it. She laughed until she ached. What in the world was she going to do!

Time passed, I'm not sure how long, before Ms. Whit regained her composure. With her one good eye, she looked the situation over and decided she would roll over to the baseboard and get in a standing position so she could take control of the situation. As it was, she felt helpless.

Taking a deep breath, she forced herself not to laugh. She had to think of the saddest thing she could remember. But now, she couldn't remember anything sad. Rolling her good eye, she looked toward the general direction of the wall and began to rock the cocoon until she got it rolling towards the baseboard. It stopped when she reached the wall. Using the tips of her bare fingers and her toes, she managed to inch her way up the board to a standing position. Balancing on her toes, Ms. Whit leaned far to the right and bumped into Robin's dish of water. Water! Of course, it was so simple. All she had to do was get inside the dish of water. She looked up and could barely see the rim of the clay bowl. Plenty of water here! Ms. Whit tried to get over the rim. She tried and she tried...then she tried again. She tried so hard. She tried to jump, she tried to hop, she even tried to leap, but she wasn't moving at all. She could see herself in the water, her mind was working brilliantly. If only her body could cooperate. She stood for a moment longer pondering the situation. With her back against the bowl, she slid to the floor, believing she could think much better if she could rest for just a minute.

She was uncomfortable. She was unable to move her arms. The cloth was getting stiffer and scratchier and drier. The situation was more dire than ever. She wanted to know what was going on inside. She wanted to go to Flatter Rock, she wanted breakfast, but most of all, she wanted out of this predicament. She dearly hoped no one from Flatter Rock or Down Below would be up to the Great Back Porch to fetch her. That would be the ultimate insult on top of the albeit painless injury. How dreadfully embarrassing. A shudder went all through her.

With that thought in mind, she was determined to find a way out. Calling on every ounce of energy she had left to her, she learned far to the right and stopped dead in her tracks.

Ms. Whit heard the padding of paws come bounding down the stairwell.

"Oh no," she groaned under her breath.

RoBin

She knew by the sound of the heavy walk that coming around the corner would be none other than the cat called Chat. It was Lord Chatterly!

Ms. Whit held her breath. Maybe he wouldn't discover her. Maybe he would simply trot on by going wherever he was going without noticing the heap of cloth with a hat and two little frog's feet poking out the bottom. Maybe she was hidden well enough that he would pass by and she would somehow slip into the water and get this awful mess off once and for all. And just maybe no one would ever have to know she tried to wipe off sticky okra juice with cheesecloth. She took another deep breath as the cat came closer.

Did I tell you? It is a common fact that Chat, finds frogs very wonderful to have for breakfast. I didn't tell you?

Oh, my dearie, it is true! Ms. Whit didn't move as Chat turned the corner. He could very well have tripped over the still form peering one-eyed through the thin cloth. Ms. Whit blinked hard and swallowed. Chat was going to pass her by. Could it possibly be he hadn't seen her? She was certain he looked straight into her good eye.

Keep going...keep going, she hoped with all her might. Just one more step and he would be off the porch. He stopped. Oh, Sweet Father MistleToad. Ms. Whit's poor little heart was racing and beat loudly in her ears. Surely the huge cat could hear it too.

Lord Chatterly stopped, he turned around and walked back to where Ms. Whit was trying desperately hard to blend into the woodwork. Why, oh why hadn't she been born a chameleon? Chat looked into her eye. She looked back into his two good ones. He closed his eyes and shook his head. This was impossible. He opened his eyes. Oh, this was too good. But it was true. He had her. After all the times he had tried to catch her unaware, this time he had her.

The monster cat sniffed at her. A low rumble started from his very paws, it seemed to Ms. Whit. A ferocious looking curl began at one corner of his massive grinning mouth. His nose wrinkled as he sniffed the length of the cheesecloth. The huge cat slowly sat back on his haunches, the grin spread across his wide furry face.

"Oh, just get it over with already! Go ahead, DO it!" Ms. Whit demanded.

Chat found the temptation irresistible. He fell to the floor holding his sides, roaring with laughter. His very well refined friend looked totally outrageous sitting in a heap, her poise askew.

Ms. Whit rolled her good eye at him. It was one thing for her to laugh at herself when no one else was looking but having to lay here helplessly watching Chat roll on the floor provided her with a different perspective. She tried to get up. He roared again. Each time she moved he went into another spasm of laughter. Ms. Whit would never be able to live this down. She could hear it now Ms.-Well-Mannered-Never-Misses-A-Step-Whit discovered on The Great Back Porch packaged like a red waxed package of Gruyere cheese.

Great MistleToad, would he ever stop? Ms. Whit looked hard at the cat. She looked hard at herself. Ms. Whit began to chuckle. Without inviting the humor, her shoulders started to shake. She felt her cheeks press against the stiff cloth. No! She would not laugh. She couldn't! It would be undignified. It would be beneath her. Seeing Chat laughing was contagious. She burst into laughter and laughed until her cheeks were sore, and she was out of breath.

A short time later, Chat sat beside his favorite breakfast companion. Didn't I tell you? Chat would rather be a vegetarian than to dine on Ms. Whit. He does not eat frogs.

The cat wiped his eyes then dabbed at Ms. Whit's one good eye, drying tears of laughter from their aching cheeks. Taking a small corner of the cheesecloth between his gleaming white teeth, Chat ever so gently lowered Ms. Whit into the bowl of water. She promptly sank to the bottom of the cool clay dish.

Chat watched as the cloth began to swell and loosen its hold from around Ms. Whit's small body. Bubbles began to form around her face then rose upward, popping as they reached the surface. Out came a tiny, wrinkled finger, then another. Finally, her hand stretched out from the gooey cover. Suddenly both hands were free and one after the other, her long slender feet.

A large bubble created an air pocket over Ms. Whit's face. Chat heard a garbled sound as it rose to the top. When the sound reached the surface he heard........"reeeeeeeee!" Ms. Whit flew over the rim of the bowl, landing neatly beside her furry feline friend.

"I'm free! I'm free!" she cried joyfully.

Chat beamed with delight as Ms. Whit reached for his face and patted him on the nose. How would she ever be able to thank him? She didn't care if he shouted the news all the way to Lake Pontchartrain, she was able to move again, able to dance a little jig, and so she did.

Ms. Whit's curiosity was winning out again as she told Chat about the events leading up to her latest adventure. Chat knew what was going on. There was little that missed the big cat's curiosity. He told her he had overheard Auntie Lo talking about a gathering coming up the next weekend.

Already there was a Passel of Humans in the kitchen. One of them had slipped on a slice of okra and gone sailing across the dining room floor crashing into Auntie Lo's wooden pie safe. Ms. Whit knew exactly when that had happened.

The question remained. Who was in the kitchen?

Adjusting the traveling bag over her shoulder, she hopped over to the stack of cheese boxes under the kitchen window and asked Chat to give her a lift. He picked her up by the strap of the bag and set her on the top box.

Resting his chin on the lid of the box, Chat stood on his hind legs while Ms. Whit scratched his cheek and patted his huge head. Lord Chatterly's purr was loud and rumbled through his chest, Ms. Whit chuckled. Pressing her cheek against his, she whispered, "thank you."

Chat gently pushed against her shoulder with his big paw, anything for her.

She watched him trot off the porch then hopped to the ledge of the freshly washed windowpane. She blinked her large eyes and touched her face to the glass. Looking into the kitchen, she watched as several of Auntie Lo's grandchildren went about clearing up the breakfast dishes and putting tins of tea and all manner of miscellaneous articles back on the shelves of the wooden pie safe.

Ms. Whit smiled. Surrounded by her grandchildren, Auntie Lo sat in the big armchair telling stories about the photographs in the heavy picture albums resting on her lap. The Humans were talking and laughing, sipping tea from the rose patterned tea set Auntie Lo saved for special occasions...which meant every day of the week.

Uncle Jackwere poured another cup of tea and sat back in his chair as the stories stirred memories he'd almost forgotten. There was so much love in the house that Uncle Jackwere built. Ms. Whit was glad she found The Great Back Porch that was attached to it.

Her curiosity satisfied at last, she absentmindedly hummed along with the music from Uncle Jackwere's radio. Caruso, I believe. Backing away from the brightly lit kitchen window, she hopped from the boxes to the edge of the step on the stairs of The Great Back Porch.

She looked around for any signs of danger. The path was clear. She took a deep breath and jumped into the grassy yard. Time to get to Flatter Rock.

Chapter Three
Flatter Rock

Hopping along the riverbank to the great rock, Ms. Whit wondered again, for the umpteenth time, how Flatter Rock got its name ...no one really knew...except that Flatter Rock had been there since forever and folks just figured it was called Flatter Rock because it was flatter than any other rock on the river and big enough to have a name. None of the other rocks had a name.

Flatter Rock was a huge rock...well, huge for a frog. It was shaded by cattails and elephant ears. A large cypress tree complemented by the thick hanging moss rose up behind the great rock and housed the many fleet-footed creatures living beside the river.

Everybody went to Flatter Rock. It was the most popular gathering place for hearing the latest news, listening to music, playing music, having a picnic, fishing, diving into TheWater, playing with tadpoles and watching dragonflies. Anyone who cared to sun or sit and watch duckweed go, wherever duckweed goes, came to Flatter Rock.

It was Tutankhamen's favorite spot and often he and Chat would venture down to the rock to lie in the sun, or watch the dance of the dragonfly, or chase the cloud shadows passing over the great flat rock.

Ms. Whit was lost in the memories of all the happy times she had spent at Flatter Rock. Her treasured visits with That Big Old BullFrog Travis, the time, only three and a half weeks ago, when Ms. Whit's Daughter...from California, had come up for a visit, and of all the many festive occasions the frogs celebrated at Flatter Rock. She wondered why though, why it seemed to take so long to get to a place where you wanted to be, but never seemed to take long at all to get back where you'd already been.

She wished she were already there...and then, suddenly, she found herself about to land in the middle of a startled crowd of related and unrelated frogs.

It wasn't as if Ms. Whit had actually traveled over the trail to Flatter Rock, she was a good distance away. She missed Possum's Crossing and June Bug Junction. She passed right over Turtle Pass and any number of the other familiar landmarks she crossed en route to Flatter Rock. She hadn't known, she hadn't been paying attention at all. She was thinking of so many other things, doing the hopping and the jumping. And lookout!

"Look out! Ohhhhhhh! Ohhhhhhh...ohhhhhh! Great Father Sweet Mistle Toady," Ms. Whit exclaimed! No time for pondering mysteries now. Plop! Ms. Whit landed smack dab in the middle of the little congregation of frogs.

They hopped backwards and stumbled over each other, whoa-ing and cavorting and looking as if somebody had popped 'em upside the head...like that famous little field mouse, they were plain taken aback. Then, as The Old BullFrog recovered from the kerfuffle, he held out a warty old, webbed hand and reached for Ms. Whit.

"Wahl, Ah do de'claya. Good mawnin' mah deah." The Big Old BullFrog drawled good naturedly."

We have been expectin' you...tho Ah must admit, yo a'rival was not an'ticipated in such uh un'convenchanal mannah'. Please, do come an' join us mah deah."

Ms. Whit took the Big Old BullFrog's hand and got up.

"Gracious me. Do forgive me everyone," Ms. Whit sheepishly proclaimed. "I...well, I must have miscalculated that last jump."

She wished she could go back the way she came, but the trouble was she didn't know how she'd done it. Miss Silky L'Polo hopped up to Ms. Whit, placing an arm around her shoulder as the other frogs nodded in understanding. It could happen to anyone as they all very well knew. It just seemed a little odd that Old Bully had spoken her name and there she was quicker than a bright blue blaze.

Well, no time to ponder this mystery. They all gathered around the Old Bullfrog and looked at him expectantly, not knowing what could come next. If frogs could shoot from the sky, no telling what the Old Bullfrog could conjure up next.

"Now, ahem," the Old BullFrog cleared his throat, "where was Ah Miss Silky?"

"You were just asking about Ms. Whit, Bully dear." Silky replied, her eyes sparkling.

There were quiet giggles and hushed laughter after that remark. No one was sure what to say. They didn't want to seem rude by laughing at someone else, so when the Big Old BullFrog chuckled low, his face breaking into a million grins, it broke the intensity of the moment, and everyone was at ease once more.

Everyone except for Ms. Whit. She blushed a deep pink and felt a distinct warmth as she looked up into the amused eyes of the venerable Old BullFrog. He was not laughing at her; she knew that was true. His laughter came from a deep well of humor filled over many years of seeing things the younger frogs had not seen. Ms. Whit was not accustomed to having attention drawn to herself for reasons other than her own doing. She never minded a joke, even at her own expense, but this was not amusing to her. She simply did not understand what had caused her to misjudge the last jump that landed her so unexpectedly amidst the small gathering of her friends. Well, there was still no time to ponder this mystery. She shook it off when everyone started talking about the next Coming up.

Now, a Coming Up is a special event. It is a celebration. Frogs will celebrate just about anything. They will celebrate visiting frogs 'coming up' from out of town. They will celebrate birthdays, anniversaries, holidays... anything that is 'coming up'.

They had a special 'Coming Up' last summer when That Big Old BullFrog's mother, Auntie Polly Woggles, who was none other than Webby Tadillia's great aunt once removed, had her one hundredth birthday.

But this next Coming Up? This wonderful, glorious, most spectacular Coming Up, was due to what was found at the inspection. Each and every time a batch of baby frogs hatch, there is someone sent in to look at their foreheads. It is a never-ending job. Baby frogs hatch every day. Inspectors are hopping from pond to river and creek to puddle to take a look. They all hoped to be the one to find the newly hatched froglette with the mark.

The inspector in this case was one Mortimer McGillacuddy. Inspector McGillacuddy spent his entire day inspecting hatchlings. He could tell at a quick glance if any baby frog had the mark.

Now do you see? That is why this Coming Up was so great. Mr. Mortimer McGillacuddy had finally found a little baby boy frog who had The Mark.

There had been many false alarms over the years, but when Mr. Mortimer had been called for the final inspection, he had always been sorely disappointed.

So, when Miss Silky and her parents had Ms. Whit call out the notice for the good inspector to come to Flatter Rock, he, Mortimer, was supremely excited. Flatter Rock was in his very own balliwac and wouldn't it be fine if the long-awaited Prince came from his very own backyard? He came for the inspection as fast as The Express could carry him. It had been a sweet day for Mortimer. He retired the very next day.

The frogs had a Coming Up when the news was made official. Ms. Whit's Daughter ...from California, was visiting at the time, and when she heard about the Coming Up, she left straight away for Texas. She went to accompany her great grandfather on his way to the Coming Up. She would tell everyone along the way there and back about the Prince. She was taking The Express and was expected to be back in time for the coronation.

Soon Miss Silky's brother, Jeremiah J. L'Polo, would be crowned Prince. As you may already be aware, the crowning of a Prince is a rare occurrence. Even Auntie Polly Woggles had only seen it on four or maybe three occasions.

Everyone had wanted to see the mark. It's an unusual mark and appears as though the little frog has been kissed upon his head or her head, by lips wearing pale pink lipstick... although, there hadn't been any little girls with the mark since anyone could remember. A princess among frogs is a rare occurrence indeed.

This Coming Up was why everyone had gathered at Flatter Rock. The residents here would be host to frogs from all over Frogdom. The turnout would be huge. That Old BullFrog had called the meeting so everyone could be assigned a part in the production of the grand event. There was so much to do and so little time. Every single member of the committee had an important role in the planning.

For example, Miss Silky and her parents were in charge of refreshments. The Big Old BullFrog was the Master of Ceremonies and Florrie Nighting-Hopper would head the decorations committee. They all did the same thing at every Coming Up. Why not? They were the best at what they did.

They had all taken a vote asking Lord Chatterly if he would bestow the honor of playing his flute. He accepted happily.

Of course, Ms. Whit was in charge of the music. It was her absolute favorite thing, her greatest passion. She loved to hear music and she loved to sing.

Knowing she would be sending the invitations out this very afternoon kept her mind off the unfortunate landing at the rock. She had all but forgotten the incident after getting caught up in all the excitement.

Now, sending out invitations is a big event too. This is how frogs get news you know. From parish to parish and county to county, frogs send news by singing it. That is what you're hearing when you are listening to Frog Songs. They're telling other frogs about the next Coming Up or some other interesting or exciting bit of news. Frogs have no phones and of course they don't write much, so they have to get the news out somehow. Of course, Humans call it croaking, but frogs know better.

That Big Old BullFrog called everyone to attention. It was time for the heralding to commence.

Chat gave the cue and blew a note on his flute. Then Tutankhamen began strummin' and thumbin' the bass, ...a chorus of little frogs started hoppin' and boppin' and Boxie opened up his case...fiddle case that is. Then the Lady Frogettes, with Miss Silky singing lead, started with the background vocals while Mildred Millipede played along on the xylophone just as pretty as you please.

Ms. Whit hopped up on That Big Old BullFrog's leg. She started snappin' her fingers and tappin' her toes. One with the music, she crooned," come , on everybody,...gather around...listen up now, 'cause we're gonna send this invitation to town!"

Come on and Join Me

Listen up...listen up...listen up all of you
Down on the river up to Down Below
There's coming up a Coming Up coming up and
That Big Old BullFrog just told me there will be singing
and dancing Escargot! Oh!
You can follow the river or catch a dillo
at the fishing dock,
You can swim, you can float, you can fly
take the boat! Bring a friend,
Bring a dish, I have only one wish
Meet me at Flatter Rock! Hey!
Come on all you lovely amphibians...
Come Turtle and Bird haven't you heard!
Well I hear Miss Silky is cookin'
and The Old BullFrog is lookin'
For Chat to be playin' his flute...
It's gonna be jazzy baby...classy too
It's a coronation, we're crowning the Prince!
So, come on and join me we're having a ball
Come on and join me come one and come all...
To...Flatter Rock....Come on and join me
Flatter Rock....At quarter past noon,
Flatter Rock....The new Prince we're crowning at
Flatter Rock....the third Saturday in June,
Flatter Rock....Flatter Rock....Flatter Rock!
Down on the river passed the fishing dock
You can hear the babies singing
Rock! Rock! Rock!
Rockity Row Boat! Rock! Rock!
Rockity Row Boat! Rock!
Go and tell your mama and don't forget your pop
Jeremiah's Coming Up he'll be at Flatter Rock!
Rockity Row Boat! Rock! Rock!
Rockity Row Boat! Rock! Rockity Rock!

Debbie Musselli 2015

Frogs hopped and leaped over the rocks and cattails, into TheWater and out, over each other and around. They played until the sun was almost set. For the little ones, it was time to go home.

Ms. Whit returned to The Great Back Porch sitting on Chat's big head. They stopped to watch the spectacular colors of the evening sky and soak up the rich fragrance of the soothing pine.

Leaning on a thick wooden post, Ms. Whit listened to the Old BullFrog singing to the night. She knew the baby frogs were listening to him, learning from the stories he sang. She sat gently rocking to the sounds of the river. Ever so softly, Ms. Whit sang a lullaby.

Ms. Whit's Lullaby

Baby...hush now baby,
Close your sleepy eyes,
(Jug-o-rum)
Oh ho hum, The Sandman comes
Sailing down the river tonight.
Baby…sleep now baby,
Mother holds you tight
Daddy guards your little heart
While you're sleeping by the river tonight
Jug-o-rum…jug-o-rum
Baby, precious baby,
Dream the whole night through,
When the shadows come,
Ho...oh...hum
I'll be here watching over you.
Good night, go to sleep
In the morning I'll wake you,
Go to sleep, close your eyes
Go to sleep my little one.
(Jug-o-rum...jug-o-rum...jug-o-rum.)

All over the riverbank, up and down, little ones went to sleep cradled in their mother's arms. Fathers rocked their babies to the soothing sounds of the river. Ms. Whit hopped to the porch swing and over to the top of her stool. Chat turned from the peaceful river, purring deeply, and rubbed his face against Ms. Whit's cheek. He padded off upstairs to sleep. Ms. Whit snuggled into her warm soft bed.

Good night, West Pearl River. Sleep tight.

Chapter Four
Just Believe

ain was falling when Ms. Whit awoke. She knew because of the large drop that splashed in her face. Ms. Whit couldn't see outside the piano stool. She didn't know how hard the rain was falling. She stretched and yawned while she crawled to the top of the hole.

Oh my! Her Beloved Piano Stool was moving! How could this be? Where was she? She looked around and did not recognize a thing...except for water. Her beloved piano stool was racing wildly down the West Pearl River!

The sky was the darkest gray and rain was pouring down in sheets. She had no idea how she'd come to be in the river or why she hadn't known a storm was coming, but in the river she was and a storm there was for certain. She looked around, but couldn't see the river's banks, only the huge trunks of the tall pine and cypress trees and rushing water.

She held on tightly, hoping the current would take her to land somewhere down river. Ms. Whit was frightened. She closed her eyes in disbelief. When she opened them, Saysa Sweet Peaches was beside her.

"Do not be afraid." the HummingBunny told her. "You did imagine your trip yesterday," Saysa Sweet Peaches smiled reassuringly, "you got to Flatter Rock by using your Imagination."

"How is that possible?" Ms. Whit asked wide-eyed, "I was only daydreaming." She wondered how Saysa Sweet Peaches could have known.

"Trust yourself, believe and you will get there." Saysa told her.

"Get there? Get where? Where is there? Where am I supposed to be going?" she shouted over the wind.

"With me," The HummingBunny told her, "Up there with me." Saysa Sweet Peaches pointed to the top of the tallest pine tree and motioned to Ms. Whit to come with her, up there.

"No, I can't fly." Ms. Whit said, "Oh HummingBunny, I know I cannot fly!"

"Follow me, all is well...you will see, only believe and you will get there."

Ms. Whit stared at the HummingBunny. A look of absolute faith was in her friend's eyes.

Everything started spinning. The gray of the sky and the rain and the river became a dizzying whirlpool. Quickly, she imagined the warmth of the HummingBunny's nest. Thoughts are things. She closed her eyes for an instant then felt the softness of cattail down. The HummingBunny was beside her, smiling.

"Oh my, oh my, oh my, I've done it!" Ms. Whit was enormously excited. "But how did I do it? Oh HummingBunny, I was there in my house, the river was flooding, and it was raining hard, I couldn't see. I was so frightened...then suddenly you were there and now I'm here. Oh! My house! Where..." Ms. Whit looked down, anxiously scanning for her beloved home.

The river ran smoothly. The sky was clear. Her beloved piano stool was nowhere to be seen. Ms. Whit blinked, dizzy from the height of the giant pine. A drop of water splashed in her face. She blinked again.

She was home. Inside the piano stool lying exactly as she did every morning. She sat up, looking around the familiar surroundings. Her traveling bag hung from the hook where she left it the night before. Her large straw hat sat beside her bed. Everything was dry.

Ms. Whit grabbed her things and hurried to the top of the hole. She looked around. It was foggy but the sprinkler was on, watering Auntie Lo's flower garden. She slipped her traveling bag over her shoulder and shoved her hat down on her head.

She must find Saysa Sweet Peaches.

She hurried along the top of the fence rail looking inside each of the morning glories, but the HummingBunny wasn't inside any of them.

She climbed down the trail of blossoms to the winecups lining the walkway and searched behind every leaf and flower. She looked up into the trees and out over the river. It was too foggy to see clearly. She called to her friend, humming the way Saysa Sweet Peaches taught her to do. No answer. She hopped down the walkway to the dock that Uncle Jackwere built, stopping every few feet to look around the Great Backyard and the river bank up and down.

"Now how am I supposed to find quicksilver in pea soup?" she said aloud to no one in particular. Ms. Whit sat down on the last lily pad on the right side of the river.

Saysa Sweet Peaches appeared out of thin air landing beside the little frog, her wings folding gently behind her. Ms. Whit didn't hear the familiar sound of the HummingBunny's arrival. She was just there.

"Oh, am I glad to see you! Just wait until you hear this...it was raining hard...the house was racing down the river...couldn't see anything but gray tree trunks and gray air, everything was gray..." Ms. Whit told the dream to the HummingBunny. Saysa listened carefully to the details, not missing a word. She nodded, she blinked, she cocked her head to one side then the other not saying a word until the very end. Then she quickly rose above Ms. Whit's head humming so fast Ms. Whit had a hard time keeping up with her. She stopped and looked directly at the little frog. Waiting for the information she had given her to sink in.

Ms. Whit sat perfectly still. She didn't breathe. She didn't dare. Only her eyes moved as she looked at the HummingBunny. Saysa Sweet Peaches lit on the lily pad beside her. Her eyes sparkled. Her face broke into a wide smile. The HummingBunny knew, now Ms. Whit knew that the HummingBunny knew.

Slowly, Ms. Whit let out a long-held breath. She looked around then back at the HummingBunny and said, "Do you know what you are saying...I do want to believe, truly I do, but how? All I know is this, frogs cannot fly." The little frog stated matter of fact.

Saysa Sweet Peaches rose from the lily pad, stretching her wings as far out as they would go. They fluttered swiftly and instantly she was hovering over Ms. Whit. Leaning towards her friend, she whispered softly, "Just believe." Then, the HummingBunny was gone.

Ms. Whit looked up at the sky, but there was not a trace of the furry winged creature that just told her she could fly. Fly! Did the HummingBunny think she was crazy enough to believe her? She must have. But could it be? The possibilities had Ms. Whit's mind racing. She had to think, she had to do something. She had to run or jump or do something that would channel the energy that was making her want to jump out of her skin.

The sun had risen some time ago. She wondered if she could find the mussels. She hopped onto the dock and looked deep into the water.

"Just believe," she said to herself as she dove head-first into the river.

Drifting slowly to the bottom, Ms. Whit found the tree stump and lit upon a root. This was something that felt familiar. This was something she knew about, something to take her mind off the wild thoughts racing through her head.

She looked at the spot where the mussels usually gathered for their morning concert. Something was different. She didn't know what, it was just different. They were different.

She looked at the strange little band and felt the oddest sensation. It seemed they were smiling at her. She had never seen them smile before...if indeed you could say mussels smile. She watched closely, wondering what they were up to. Ms. Whit smiled back at them.

This was an unusual welcome. The mussels weren't afraid. They didn't even seem the least bit shy. She swam over to them. They began making a strange clicking sound, smiling at her all the while. She could not imagine what it was they were trying to tell her.

She swam to a little patch of grass on the river's floor and, holding on to a thick, long blade she watched. Soon, she heard a tiny little voice begin to sing. She tried peering over the clump of grass but didn't see anything. She parted the grass and saw a wee mussel baby. The baby was singing.

Ms. Whit closed her eyes as the melody passed through TheWater and flooded her ears with the magical sounds of the music the mussels make.

The melody was so familiar, yet she knew she had never heard this song from the mussels before. She listened then began to hum along.

After the tiny mussel baby and Ms. Whit had been singing for a little while, she remembered. The place she heard the music before was above TheWater, from Uncle Jackwere's radio. There was an entire orchestra performing the piece when she heard it before. She remembered humming along with the radio. The duet she sang now was the same melody but she wasn't just hearing it. She was feeling it. It was the most delightful sound she had ever felt. She wished Uncle Jackwere could feel the music from the radio here at the bottom of the river.

When the song was over, Ms. Whit kissed the baby mussel on the shell then waved good-bye to her friends. She hurried to the surface for air.

"Believe," she thought again as she pulled herself up on the lily pad. Just believe.

Thoughts are things.

Ms. Whit grabbed her traveling bag and hopped onto the dock. Just like clockwork, Boxie Tortusie and his siblings were sunning on the dock.

"Good morning Ms. Whit!" She heard it once, twice, three times, four.

"Good morning Teodoro, good morning Michaelito, good morning Giuseppe, good morning Boxie, it's a glorious morning isn't it!" she cheerfully replied.

"Bela! Bela, you gotta believa deep inna you hearta,." Boxie answered as he walked off the deck into TheWater.

"Boxie, what did you say?" Ms. Whit asked, startled by his answer. She started back to the dock to ask him what he meant, but Boxie's head disappeared into TheWater.

Teodoro's head popped out of TheWater,

"Believe it!" Michaelito's head popped out of TheWater,

"Believe it!" "Believe in yer own self," Giuseppe's small voice yelled before going under.

Ms. Whit watched them swim away. Halfway across the river, Boxie turned to smile at the frog.

What did Boxie know? Was this simply a strange coincidence, she wondered. It seemed there was many a strange thing happening on The West Pearl River.

Chapter Five
Jake, the Slingshot, and Danny

Ms. Whit was still pondering Boxie's remark, hopping down the riverbank on her way to have brunch at Flatter Rock. She noticed the breeze blowing through the grass and felt it as she crossed the stones. The sun was just the right touch of warm. It was a gorgeous morning. She felt like she was floating over the riverbank when she saw a group of Auntie Lo's grandchildren skimming rocks across the river. She stopped under a vine of ivy and hid behind a leaf to watch them for a while.

Not all Humans knew about frogs. Sometimes, some people were not nice to frogs. Some Humans didn't understand there is a connection between every living thing. They don't understand or have a healthy respect or love of nature and because not everyone understood, Ms. Whit kept her distance.

She saw several of the grandchildren wander off to other parts of The Great Backyard. She would wait a little longer before continuing her trip to Flatter Rock. She didn't want these Humans to see her. She didn't want to wind up in some grandchild's pocket, or worse, some old smelly pickle jar for a grandchild's show and tell.

She heard the awful stories from her papa. Her great-great-great-great Grandmother Emily was caught by a Human many long years ago. She spent weeks in a jar in a classroom living off awful dead bugs and smelly tap water. No grass, no trees, no river. Some kind soul had finally taken her to the West Pearl River and let her go by a thick clump of cattails. Grandmother Emily had told the story over and over again. It was then passed down for many generations.

Ms. Whit saw one of the biggest kids take a slingshot from his back pocket and load it with one of the rocks from the pile the grandchildren had gathered.

"Hey Jake, watch this!" yelled Danny.

Jake looked up from the trail of ants he was watching carry off a large crust of bread he threw down for them earlier. He looked to where Danny was aiming the slingshot.

"Wait, Danny! Don't shoot!" Jake jumped up running as the big kid stretched the band back as far as it would go and let the stone fly.

Swoosh! Thunk! The stone ripped through a small bird's nest scattering feathers and twigs over the ground under the tree. What was left of the nest came falling to the pine needle covered ground shot in pieces.

Jake reached the other kid as the nest hit the ground.

"Danny, what are you doing? Are you crazy? You can't go around shooting bird's around here." Jake tried to push the slingshot away before Danny could load it and shoot anything else.

"Aw go on." said Danny. "It's just an old nest, ain't no birds live in it anyways...and what's the big idea you tryin' t'take my slingshot hunh?"

"Take your slingshot? You are crazy...who'd want your old slingshot anyway? You just can't go around shooting everything you want to, that's all. It ain't right, it just ain't right,." Jake told him.

Danny stood toe to toe with Jake. "Oh yeah, who says I can't shoot a old bird's nest hunh?"

Jake looked up at Danny. He thought of all the things Uncle Jackwere had taught him about The Great Backyard. That to Uncle Jackwere, this was nature's sanctuary. Jake's love for Uncle Jackwere and The Great Backyard was greater than his fear of the big kid who might destroy it. Jake knew in his heart he was right. He squared his thin narrow shoulders and leaned towards Danny. Jake was not about to budge.

"I said." Jake told him firmly.

Danny started to shove the other boy, but something in the way Jake spoke let Danny know he wasn't afraid. Instead of shoving the boy, he shoved the slingshot back into his pocket.

"Aw go on and play house with the girls," Danny sneered as he spun on one foot and took off for his own backyard.

Jake stood for a minute and watched the big kid walk away. He was sure there for a minute that Danny had every intention of punching him in the face...or something. He walked over to the pile of rocks and started skipping them across TheWater as he thought it all through. Jake wasn't sure why Danny had let him go so easily, but if being right was what convinced Danny, then Jake was sure glad he'd been right. He was glad he stood up to him too. Aw, he knew Danny wasn't a bad kid. It was just that Jake's ideas and Danny's ideas were different. Danny might think it was OK to shoot nests and other stuff, but for Jake it wasn't OK. It didn't feel right to him. Couldn't Danny find something better to shoot at?

It irked Jake that Danny would do something like that and not think about the consequences. What if everybody went around shooting all the bird's nests out of all the trees? And what if everyone went around shooting the birds, or all the windows just because they liked hearing the glass break and cats because they were meowing or dogs because they howled or your Aunt Mary's flower garden or anything they wanted to shoot anytime they wanted to shoot it? Why, pretty soon, there would be chaos in the world. It wouldn't be safe to walk out your own front door without fear of being pinged by a slingshot, or worse.

No, there had to be rules. He understood and he thought Danny would too. He would talk to Danny later on. He was sure he could get Danny to at least see his position. Then it would be up to Danny to decide if following rules was a bad thing or a good thing. Jake hoped Danny would decide to listen to his side and maybe they could set up a shooting range. Jake knew one thing for certain; Danny was a very good shot.

Ms. Whit knew that not every human understood the connection there was between every living thing, but it still startled her to see the Human shoot the nest from the tree. She was glad it was empty and shuddered to think what could have happened had there been baby birds inside.

She watched Jake drift off towards the house. She liked that Human, but it would be a snowy day in August in The Great Backyard of Slidell, Louisiana before she understood Humans like Danny. In fact, she didn't think she ever could.

She started off for Flatter Rock again. This time the trip was uneventful. She passed The Big Old BullFrog's Hollow and watched a family of ducks waddle through Possum's Crossing. She wondered how

Deb Musselli 2015

she had missed them yesterday then remembered her dream and the words of Saysa Sweet Peaches. Just believe? If she did all that by just believing she could do it, she wished she knew how she believed it. It seemed to her that if a body were able to travel to places without actually moving anywhere, they at least ought to know how. Why couldn't she do it now? Why did she still have to walk or hop or jump?

There just never was time enough to ponder the mysteries she was discovering. She hopped onto the big stone where Tutankhamen and Lord Chatterly were napping under the warming sun. Chat's head rested on Tutankhamen's back; his ear twitched at the touch of a dragonfly landing there. The strange duo didn't move as Ms. Whit hopped noiselessly to the edge of the rock. She removed her traveling bag and her hat then jumped into the river.

Chapter Six

Grander and Ms. Whit's Daughter... from California

rander and Ms. Whit's Daughter...from California, arrived at Flatter Rock some while after Ms. Whit jumped into TheWater.

Whooping and hollering, Grander made their arrival known to the entire neighborhood, nearly scaring Chat into only eight lives. Tutankhamen on the other hand, only opened his bleary eyes, yawned and went back to sleep. Nothing short of Mr. Hawthorne's dog could rouse Tutankhamen from his morning nap.

Daphne, Mr. Hawthorne's huge brindle colored English Mastiff, was an absolute pest to Tutankhamen because Daphne loved to play with Tutankhamen.

Boxie had warned him about Daphne long ago saying, "Keepa outa d'way fromma dat bigga doga.".

That was all Tutankhamen needed until the day Daphne caught him off guard and managed to get him on his back and spin him around until his eyes crossed.

For now, Daphne was nowhere around so Tutankhamen barely heard Grander and Ms. Whit's Daughter...from California, when they arrived at Flatter Rock.

Chat greeted the two travelers, inviting them to sit and visit until Ms. Whit returned. Her traveling bag was on the rock so she couldn't be far. She was probably visiting Down Below, Chat figured.

They sat on the rock to wait and talked about the trip from Choke Canyon and the Coming Up and the crowning of the new Prince. Of course, it wasn't long before Chat pulled his flute out from under the edge of the big rock and began to play.

Not long after that, Grander began to sing. He sang opera stuff. Not traditional opera, for not too many of the cowboys who lived with him on the ranch in Choke Canyon understood "regular" opera, although some of them understood a little. So Grander sang Cowboy Opera. His voice was magnificent. He sang tenor with a touch of a country twang...but just a touch mind you. Enough to be considered country by the other Cowboys.

At first, Grander had a hard time convincing them that the songs he sang had anything to do with Cowboys. But, over the years he'd done just that. He improvised and made up his own words to some of the most well-known operatic arias ever written. It worked out splendidly.

The Cowboys loved to hear him sing. So did the coyotes and the cows and even the chickens around the ranch house. It is well documented that the Rancher's hens laid more and better eggs than anywhere else in the county. Yup, everyone loved to hear Grander sing. So, when Chat brought out his flute, Grander just naturally sang along.

Now, I don't know how many times you've heard a cat playing a flute or an old Texas frog singing Cowboy Opera, but I can assure you it is a most uncommon sight. Grander sang his favorite song. It sorta sounded like that great old song O Sole Mio...sorta. It reminds Grander of the time he spent in The City. He had heard that great Master sing the song in Italian. He wanted the Cowboys to hear it, so he changed the words and learned to sing it without the music.

My Palomino

When I ride the Wind
with the sun on my back
My heart goes to soaring
through the Canyon's end
The wind is roaring
and we go exploring again
Just me and my Palomino
Golden in the sun
riding the Canyon
from sunrise 'til day is done
My friend by my side
for the rest of my life
a truer love is rare
for when I'm alone
so far from home
My Palomino is there
My friend
My friend, it's true
Heaven's at hand
When stars like these shine
Bright is the future
This is our time,
Now is our time to ride
Ride and be free
My Palomino and me
My friend
My friend Thistle-Lee

Chapter Seven
Believing Begins

s. Whit left Flatter Rock to have brunch with Miss Silky and Auntie Toadie McRoadie. Auntie Toadie McRoadie lived across the river from Down Below underneath a huge patch of hydrangeas in a large, chipped clay pot turned upside down and wedged into the riverbank.

Toadie McRoadie came from Scotland on a cruise ship bound for New York City. She got lost on the voyage and wound up in Louisiana. She never regretted the mix up and came to love the West Pearl River, considering it her home as much as if she'd been born there.

Silky and Auntie Toa were going over the menu Silky's mother had prepared for the Coming Up when Ms. Whit came jaunting through the doorway.

Good morning to ye Dear One," Auntie Toa exclaimed, hopping up and giving Ms. Whit a hug.

"Come in! Come in lass. It's a rough time y've been havin'. I heard of yer plop yes't'dy. Tis' a pity ye ken. So, do tell me now, what is ailin' you my bonnie lass? Have you the auge...have you the rumitoid, are you having plenty of fiber in yer diet, ...are you sleepin' well? Come now, you can tell Toa. What is ailing you Dear One? Hmm?"

Ms. Whit was momentarily stricken speechless. She had not considered any of the maladies Auntie Toa had mentioned. She didn't have 'the auge' at least she didn't think so. 'The rumitoid' sounded like a condition for the Humans' and Ms. Whit got plenty of fiber in her diet.

She returned the hug to Auntie Toa and said, "Oh my, Toa, I don't believe I have any of those little things the matter. I was doing a little daydreaming and not paying attention is all. Really, there is no need to worry." She sat down at the tiny table where Silky was looking over the menu. "Good morning Silky dear, how are your parents?" she inquired.

"Mama and Papa are gathering today," said Silky. "Mama wanted to get a head start on some things, so she's asked me to come get recipes from Auntie Toa, she's such a dear." Silky looked fondly at her friend.

"Splendid, that's a good idea. Toa has the best recipes," Ms. Whit agreed. "Your Mama is smart to start so early. Now what did I interrupt you two scallywags doing this fine morning?"

"Auntie Toa was going over the menu with me, you know how I adore her Scottish brogue. I have asked her to read it to me again and read the recipes too. Would you like for her to start again so you can hear it all?" Silky asked.

"Please do Toa, ye ken we love to hear you talk. Truly we do." Ms. Whit gave her best Scottish brogue imitation.

"Aye lassies, I dunnu' wha' you are speakin' aboot...speech is speech. Sayin' Tar Tar sauce is sayin' Tar Tar sauce is it not?"

They giggled at Auntie Toa. The three were the best of friends. They met every week for brunch. Every other Tuesday, they met at Silky's house. Every other Wednesday, they met at Auntie Toa's and every other Friday, they met at Ms. Whit's on The Great Back Porch and dined on ice cold hot pink lemonade and Ribbitz toast covered with pine seed butter and persimmon marmalade. In Ms. Whit's estimation, there was nothing finer than Ribbitz and marmalade. All the other days they met at Flatter Rock.

However, she admitted, Auntie Toa had outdone herself with these tiny finger sandwiches. There was water cress seasoned with a taste Ms. Whit did not recognize. There was dandelion tea and blackberry compote on angel wing tarts. She reached for her second finger sandwich when she heard the yell.

Three little heads popped up from the table. Ms. Whit beamed broadly.

"Grander!" she cried. "I'd know that holler anywhere, I must be off now. Thank you, Toa, it's been wonderful. Silky, come to Flatter Rock as soon as you can." She rushed out the doorway blowing kisses to her friends. Jumping into the water, she heard Auntie Toa call to her.

"...and be sartin' t'tell yer dear Grandsire hallew fer me Ms. Whit mi leannain!"

Ms. Whit soared through TheWater. She thought of Grander, 'thoughts are things' and in just a few split seconds she was there. She hopped upon a lily pad then straight onto the rock amidst Chat and Grander entertaining a large group of frogs who had gathered on the rock.

Grander was singing about Thistle-Lee. Thistle-Lee is Grander's horned toad. Grander calls her the Golden Palomino of Horned Toads, after the mare at the ranch at Choke Canyon. Thistle-Lee and Grander have been riding the range together for a very long time.

Grander hates to be without her, but he and Ms. Whit's Daughter...from California, flew The Express back to Slidell, so Thistle-Lee had to stay back at the ranch.

Ms. Whit knew the song Grander sang by heart. On the last verse she joined him in the song. When the song was finished, Ms. Whit jumped into her Grandfather's arms.

"Grander!" she exclaimed for the second time that day.

"AnnaBelle! Yer shore a sight fer sore eyes young'un'." Grander grinned widely.

He removed his faded cowboy hat and kissed his granddaughter's cheek.

"M-o-t-h-e-r!" Ms. Whit's Daughter...from California, cried, hopping up onto the big rock.

Ms. Whit spun around to see her daughter...from California, and shouted excitedly, "My darling daughter!"

The little frogs hopped over to each other and hugged each other tight. They hopped about then hugged then hopped about again.

"Like Mother, we have just spent the most unbelievable seven days of my life in the company of c-o-w-s. Huge hairy, beasts mother. Cows smell like, like cows. Mother, there were a zillion of them on great grandfather's ranch. Mama, have you ever seen a c-o-w up close? Oh-my-gosh! Cows are like as big as the m-o-o-n. We rode on one of Grander's cows. Actually, rode right on her horn. We rode all around the ranch and saw every coyote and javelina hog, every cactus and road runner and oh my goodness that is a huge ranch! It took me three days just to find Grander when I first arrived. But my, we had a grand time getting here. It's been a wonderful trip and I am so happy to see you."

"It's great you had a new adventure; adventures can open up brand new worlds to explore and I am so pleased you made it back in time for the Coming Up," said Ms. Whit."

"Well, I reckon we couldn't a missed it." Grander drawled. "I been meanin' t'get back to Loo'zianna fer quite a spell now, seemed a good time t'see alla y'all, so me 'n this young'un caught us a ride back on that Express service this little filly went to fetch me on. It do declare, it sure beats all I ever did see. I ain't never been so high up. That Mayla is a pure delight. Entertaining as a kitten with a Katydid I reckon. Used to take pert near a month to get here. Well, I am right glad t'be here. So how is the Old Toadie girl doin' anyway."

"Splendidly Grander, she sends her love," Ms. Whit replied. "Ever since her visit to Texas she's been looking for a horned toad!"

Grander chuckled. The memory of Toadie on Thistle-Lee was a humorous thing. Toadie had grit though. She'd make a fine cowgirl if ever she'd get out of the big city of Slidell. There was nothing like country living and Choke Canyon was about as country as you could get.

Up the riverbank came That Big Old BullFrog with Webby Tadillia, Tutankhamen and a half a dozen others. Hearing Grander yell had caused quite a fuss, and they all wanted to be at Flatter Rock for the grand reunion.

The little frogs swam under the shade of the big rock listening to their elders. It wouldn't be long before they joined them on the banks of the river.

Tutankhamen opened his eyes. In the distance, the loud sharp barking of Mr. Hawthorne's huge English Mastiff was getting closer and closer to the river. Tutankhamen didn't say a word. He rose from the rock, walked over to the edge and disappeared into the river.

Everyone laughed.

HECHO EN
MEXICO

Chapter Eight

The News from Saysa Sweet Peaches

Grander's cowboy opera attracted boatloads ...little bitty ones, of visitors to the big rock. Soon there was a full-fledged party going on. Frogs hopped about the rock until late into the night.

When the last firefly gave out and went to bed, Ms. Whit excused herself from the party. With hugs and kisses all around, she headed for The Great Back Porch.

Thoughts are things.

She needed time to think things through. She hopped partway up the riverbank then sat down in the middle of Big Old BullFrog's Hollow. Exhausted, she looked far down the riverbank to The Great Back Porch. The light was still on. It seemed so far away, if only...home, she thought. Instantly, she was inside her beloved piano stool.

Was believing you could do it really all there was to it? She had been thinking about it since yesterday. She understood the simplicity of believing in yourself, so why had she been so afraid? Hadn't she proven what she could do simply by believing she could?

She remembered how badly she wanted to be with Grander when she heard his yell. She believed she could do it, so she did it. She had used her imagination to get wherever she wanted to be. And tonight, she wanted to be home...here it was, proof again. Just believe the HummingBunny told her. So, she believed and here she was. It was true for her. She believed it into being.

It was all so new to her. It seemed accidental the way she plopped into the middle of everyone yesterday. But today was no accident and tonight was absolutely premeditated.

Is this the way it was supposed to happen, she wondered? Were there no bolts of lightning, no celebrations, no parades, no one to say you have reached your goal, you have arrived!

Ms. Whit could fly just by using her Imagination. The idea was astonishing. The fact that it was true excited her beyond belief. So why was she still afraid?

She sat on her bed pondering all these things when she heard a noise outside. Donning her hat, she wriggled up the hole.

Saysa Sweet Peaches was waiting for her, flitting quickly about and humming fast.

"What is it Saysa?" Ms. Whit came out and sat on the stool top.

Saysa Sweet Peaches said she went chasing the wind, looking for a storm. She found it. It was heading for the Gulf of Mexico. It will come soon, maybe here.

They talked about the storm, about Ms. Whit's adventures. Saysa Sweet Peaches knew her friend was discovering great wonders. She knew she would find out on her own what HummingBunnies already knew. First you must believe in yourself. That is the only magic there is to all of everything.

"Take care of yourself my friend," Saysa told Ms. Whit as she hovered over her. "You cannot save them all. Remember, just believe. Believe in yourself." And in the blink of an eye, Saysa Sweet Peaches was gone.

Ms. Whit wondered what the HummingBunny meant. Save all of what or whom? She didn't want to save anybody. All she wanted was sleep. Crawling back down the hole of the piano stool, she snuggled into her bed and dreamed about chasing storms and flying.

Chapter Nine

Before the Strom

s. Whit sat on the edge of the stone and called everyone to Flatter Rock. She didn't wait long before they began arriving. When there was a good size crowd gathered, she told them about the storm.

Some would get as far away from the river as they could possibly get. Some would stay and brave the wind and rain and flying objects. Others would simply dig a hole, crawl in and ignore the whole thing. Sometimes that worked out fine, as it would for mussels and such. For others, like frogs and turtles, ignoring storms wasn't such a good idea. They would have to use their instincts to find a place to keep safe from the hurricane.

All creatures have a sense about storms and such. They already know what to do. They know they can't stop a storm, so they don't fret about storms. They don't worry when it is hot out, they don't worry when it is cold. You won't ever hear a frog complain about the weather.

So, they went about their business just like any other day. They had breakfast and swam in the river. They told the little frogs about the storm and showed them where to go when it was time to get to a safe place. They played and hopped about doing frog things while the storm moved closer to the coast.

Now, Humans on the other hand get ready for hurricanes in a different manner altogether. Humans need to protect their homes from high winds and heavy rains, so they nail plywood over windows and put things away that could be blown away or otherwise removed during a storm.

Uncle Jackwere was nailing sheets of plywood over the windows of The Great House. There wasn't much going on except for the pounding of the hammers and the grandchildren playing in The Great Backyard.

The neighbor's boy Danny was back again. His sling shot in his pocket. He played with Jake and the other boys, building forts and castles from the pile of bricks stacked by the grill Uncle Jackwere kept meaning to enlarge.

Auntie Lo was in the kitchen preparing lunch. Her nieces helped her make grilled cheese sandwiches; they had fresh tomatoes from the garden. There were cucumbers and snap beans cooked with onions, sweet cornbread and for dessert pineapple upside down cake. Auntie Lo made fresh lemonade with strawberry puree.

They called the grandchildren and the menfolk in to eat. The children trotted in to wash up while Uncle Jackwere and his son finished nailing off the last sheet of plywood.

Danny was supposed to have gone home. Uncle Jackwere was about to climb down the ladder when he heard the thwack of a stone hit way high up in a pine tree. He turned around and saw the tail end of a blue shirttail dart behind the farthest tree. Falling onto the dock was something Uncle Jackwere had never seen before. He didn't know it was a tiny wreath of tender grapevines stuffed with cattail down.

The weatherman on the radio was covering the storm closely. Every thirty minutes, there was an update on Hurricane Debra. It would reach the Gulf of Mexico by nightfall. People living in Texas, Louisiana, Mississippi,

Alabama, and Florida and Georgia were under severe weather warnings for the next forty-eight hours.

The sky was starting to darken. The wind was picking up. The air smelled like rain and there was a chill in it that felt good after the heat and heavy humidity of the morning.

Walking out to the fishing dock, Uncle Jackwere decided to take one more look around. He looked out over the West Pearl River. He knew it could flood and may cause a good deal of damage, but everything he could do had been done. It was time to head for higher ground.

Uncle Jackwere glanced down at the boardwalk and bent to pick something off the boards. It was a nest of some sort. He turned it around and around. He had never seen a nest like this before. He put it inside his shirt pocket and headed back to The Great House.

He was sure he knew how the nest wound up on the boardwalk. Slingshots were pesky things. Uncle Jackwere hadn't any use for them. He had to admit though...Danny was a very good shot.

Reaching The Great Back Porch where he'd nailed some birdhouses to the wall, he lifted the latch that held the roof on one house and placed the nest inside. He'd show it to the others when they got back home. It was time to get on the road. There were only a few hours before the storm reached the coast and made landfall. He wanted to be as far away from home as he could get. There were friends they could stay with that were high and dry, but it would take a good few hours to reach them. As soon as they ate their lunch the Humans headed for higher ground.

Sometime later, we're not sure how long Ms. Whit left Flatter Rock with Grander and Ms. Whit's Daughter...from California, accompanying her. They hopped down the riverbank heading for the Great Back Porch. They decided it would be the best place for the three of them to hole up during the storm. Hopping and jumping their way to the little birdhouse nailed to the wall on The Great Back Porch, one by one they slipped through the small round entryway. Ms. Whit's Daughter...from California, was the first to enter.

"Oh...my...stars! It's like w-a-r-m. ...Mother, come see, what is this?"

Ms. Whit popped her head inside the hole. When her eyes became adjusted to the dark she said, "Well Darling...I suppose it's a ...well it's a..."

""Hummin'Bunny nest," Grander said, finishing Ms. Whit's sentence as he popped his head inside the house. "Yep, cain't cha smell it? Smells like fresh air, pine trees and honey, Grander explained. "This here nest b'longs to a little feller 'bout knee high to a horny toad, call 'em Hummin'Bunnies. I ain't seen one in prit near a ki'yote's age. I wonder where it came from."

"I know where it came from Grander," Ms. Whit told her Grandfather, "But I don't know how it got here." Ms. Whit's Daughter...from California, looked at her mother and her great grandfather. "W-e-l-l, like this is totally radical...fer sure...but like what is a HummingBunny?"

BOOM! Thunder crashed. BOOM! BOOM! Again, and again it cracked and roared. The thunder and lightning heralded the storm's arrival. It pelted every single square centimeter of every surface it could touch with tiny stinging bullets of rain. The wind howled through every crack and tiny hole of the little house. Lightning flashed a warning of the upcoming peal of thunder. Tree limbs danced wildly and beat against

Joy
Peace
Love
HoPE

the eaves and roof of The Great House, casting shadows of bizarre dancers across the walls. The birdhouse shook and rattled but held firmly to The Great Back Porch. The wind whistled through the entryway.

"That's a f-i-n-e answer!" shouted Ms. Whit's Daughter...from California, her words were lost in the deafening noise of the storm.

The tiny trio couldn't hear over the din, so they snuggled close together, warm and cozy in the little nest belonging to the HummingBunny.

It was strange. Hurricanes were not often accompanied by thunder and lightning. Hurricanes don't often have the vertical winds to create the electrical fields needed to make lightning and thunder. This was indeed a super storm.

Hours passed. They took turns looking out the entry. Flashes of lightning lit this darkest of nights into the brightest day. Occasionally, the wind would whip one of them back into the nest as if to remind them who it was in charge.

On one of Ms. Whit's ventures to the entryway, she grabbed hold of the edge of the opening and leaned into the wind. It was gloriously cold. She strained her eyes and ears waiting for the flash of lightning to show her The Great Backyard. It was unbelievable. Ms. Whit had seen in that brief instant the fury of the hurricane. The powerful storm tossed objects about as if they were made of papier maché. Lightning struck again. She hopped back into the nest and shivered from the cold.

From somewhere deep in the storm, Ms. Whit heard a voice. She looked at the two frogs beside her. They hadn't seemed to notice. She heard the voice again. Surely it was her imagination because no one would be out in a storm like this.

She snuggled into the warm nest and closed her eyes. Hearing the voice again, she opened her eyes. She didn't hear anything. Once more she closed her eyes and tried to snuggle into the downy nest. Again, she heard the voice. She looked at her two companions sitting snug in the nest. They didn't appear to be hearing anything out of the ordinary. Turning over on her side, she hoped a different position would keep her ears from playing tricks on her. She stared at the opening of the birdhouse. Nothing. She closed her eyes, but again heard the voice.

"Don't either of you hear that voice?" she shouted.

The three little frogs looked at one another. This time they all heard the voice.

Ms. Whit hopped to the entryway waiting for the next flash of lightning. She gasped aloud, "Auntie Toa!"

"Haa...a...lew...ew," came the voice, sounding as if it came from inside the hurricane. "Haaaaaleeewww ta' houuussse,." Auntie Toa called again.

Ms. Whit's Daughter...from California, and Grander scrambled to the entry as Ms. Whit looked out the hole.

"Ot Lahst, ot lahst...Saints be praised." Auntie Toadie McRoadie was exhausted as she stuck her bedraggled face into the house, croaking out one last, "Haaleww."

Grander and Ms. Whit grabbed hold of Auntie Toa's chilled hands and tried to pull her through the hole.

"I'm stuck lass, do try again, I'm on m'lahst leg...I cannu' go farther I'm sartin." Auntie Toa lamented

"Breathe out hard old gal," Grander told her.

Auntie Toa took one long deep breath and exhaled as hard as she was able. With a slight sucking noise, she came through the entryway, landing on the others inside the nest.

"Oh! Auntie Toa, you poor dear!" cried Ms. Whit as she scrambled up off the floor. "Are you alright...are you hurt anywhere...what brings you out on an awful night like this?"

Auntie Toa shook from head to toe, her small body chilled inside out. She tried to speak but was chattering so badly she couldn't get a word out.

Ms. Whit's Daughter...from California, wrapped a cover around Auntie Toa's shoulders and before long, her trembling began to ease.

"Th-th-thank you l-lassie. Aye, tis a frightful nigh' ta' be oot n' aboot, boot I cou'na keep from it. Tis the coomin' Prince it tis. Young Jeremiah is missin' froom t'others n' we kin no' look for ta poor laddy for t'river's too high. I've been tryin' t'reach ye fer hours it tis, only I kep bein' blown off m'course and havin' ta start over again."

"Jeremiah's missing? Great Father MistleToad! What can we do?"

Ms. Whit was dumbfounded. What could any of them possibly do to help Jeremiah in a storm like this?

"Oh...my....stars! What happened Toa? Did anyone like, see anything?" Ms. Whit's Daughter...from California, yelled against the wind.

"Aye lass, t'river, Jeremiah 's gone down t'river." answered Auntie Toa.

Down the river? Jeremiah's gone? It was impossible. He's to be the new Prince. He was destined to be the new leader. He wasn't supposed to be lost in the river. He couldn't be lost. Ms. Whit sat down hard on the rim of the nest. She had to think. She had to think of some way she could save Jeremiah. This was unbelievable.

Outside the safety of the little house, lightning flashed and thunder crashed. The wind howled and rain beat down in torrents upon every single thing in The Great Backyard and on The Great House and on The Great Back Porch. Nothing escaped the wrath of the storm.

Gaining her strength, Auntie Toa spoke again. "T'was Silky saw 'im lahst. She said it a'ppeared that Jeremiah was tryin' ta get soomthin' off a tree limb it was...soomthin' snarled in the branch...we cou'na make oot what...young Jeremiah's Da went to help boot tha poor dear was tangled in da wire n' twisted his great leg, he's hart, I cou'na tell how bad. Boot we war all agreein' it would be t'best fer me to coom for you Ms. Whit m'darlin...so here I am... boot what's ta do?" Her poor tired shoulders drooped as she hung her head and sighed deeply. The dear old Scottish spirit in her was drained by the storm and worry for the Prince.

Ms. Whit climbed to the entrance of the birdhouse. She was crazy to think there was anything she could do. Who could help? She felt all alone. She had to think. Auntie Toa had made it here, but...how long had it taken her to get across The Great Backyard? Hours and hours? Anything could have happened to Jeremiah by now. He could be anywhere. He could be miles from here. Where would she even begin to look? How would she get to him?

Oh, Great MistleToad, ...what was she supposed to do? The storm was flooding the banks of the West Pearl River, the coming Prince was lost, there was a hurricane still raging with a terrific force, and she was but a tiny frog clinging to the entrance of a little birdhouse. All she had was determination and what courage she could muster to face the darkness of her fear. Oh yes, she was afraid.

Grander put his arm around his granddaughter. "It's an amazin' thing ya know." Even as he yelled into her ear, she could barely hear him.

Ms. Whit wiped the tears from her face as she turned to face her grandfather. "What is amazing Grander?" she yelled in his ear.

"Why believin' is amazin'," he answered her. "Believin' in yerself and believin' in yer own courage," he continued. "Jeremiah did somethin' he must'a believed in pritty highly to go off n' be out in a floodin' river. His Daddy did somethin' he believed in..."

"And busted his leg in the effort" she reminded him."

"At's true enough, sometimes thar's a hitch er two comes with believin'," Grander said, his eyes twinkling. "Yup, just a couple a hitches now n' agin'. Sometimes courage is a mighty hard thing to muster in the eye of bein' afraid," Grander explained.

"Oh Grander, I don't know that I believe in my courage. It takes more to do it than just believing you can! I know it can be done, I'm just not sure I can do it. I believe in your courage. You could do it Grander, but me, I'm so scared. Why can't I just let whatever happens...happen. I really don't have a choice...do I…I could just say it was the storm that did it...a little old frog couldn't go up against a storm, everyone would understand...it wasn't me...poor Jeremiah...it was the storm." She looked out the doorway. "I almost believe I could find Jeremiah. It's just that ...well, I... I'm afraid. There is a hurricane here...right now...it's not just coming, it's here. It's a wild night to be out. It's the wind and the rain...and, oh everything! I don't know..." She looked at him, tears welling up in her eyes.

Grander put his arms around his granddaughter's shoulders. They looked out into the night. Lightning flashed again and again the thunder roared.

Grander leaned close to Ms. Whit's ear. "If ya don't go, ya won't never know. You've learnt somethin' I ain't see'd in a long, long while. You got somethin' rare, I see'd it in yer eyes when we first flew in on that dad burned Heron ex'press. I was gonna talk to ya 'bout it, after the Crownin'. But now seems like as good a time as any. Cain't none of us tell the future. Cain't a'one of us say what's a'gonna happen if you go through that door. But I know this t'be sure fire. Yew kin do more than yew have imagined so far...I promise ya that."

Suddenly Ms. Whit remembered her dream. She knew it was only a dream, but with every fiber of her thin little being and the wonderful words that Grander told her and all the wonders she had been experiencing, she knew she may very well be the future of the Frog Prince. She knew that very moment she had to attempt to make a difference. Nobody can make you get up and try. You do it or you don't do it. You must make a choice. The outcome is not always predictable. Doing nothing is a choice. She chose to do something. She yelled at the frogs in the birdhouse.

"I'm going to find Jeremiah!" Ms. Whit reached for the open doorway. I do believe, I can fly.

"Saints be with you Ms. Whit m'leannain!" Auntie Toa exclaimed.

"Jest yew remember, yew kin do more'n yew ever imagined!" Grander reassured her.

"Mother! Wait! You cannot go! You'll be smashed to pieces! Oh Mother! You'll be in the gravest danger and there are highwaymen and robbers and what about the a-l-l-i-g-a-t-o-r-s! Oh Mother...please... please don't go! I would miss you so if the alligators come, M-o-t-h-e-r! I love you Mother!" cried Ms. Whit's Daughter…from California.

Ms. Whit held onto her hat as she balanced herself on the perch of the little birdhouse. She looked back at her Daughter...from California, she told her she loved her. The wind sent a cold chill down her back. She had no time to think. Lightning flashed. The wind whipped through The Great Backyard, howling fiercely. Ms. Whit was gone.

Chapter Ten
After the Storm

t had been hours since Ms. Whit disappeared from the perch of the small birdhouse. Her Daughter...from California, watched through the hole of the entryway. She could see a faint glow of light through the hole. Grander and Auntie Toadie rested in the warm nest.

The wind had stopped howling. Thunder only rumbled in the distance as Hurricane Debra passed through the parish. They would all have to deal with the aftermath, clearing the debris and righting the upside down wreckage, getting everything back to the way it was before the storm.

Climbing out onto the perch where her mother had been hours before, Ms. Whit's Daughter...from California, was in awe of the scene below.

"Oh...... my s-t-a-r-s. Grander, Auntie Toa, come see this. This is, like, unbelievable. All the water in the world is running down the river. It's up to the porch. We'll be underwater if it gets much deeper."

Grander and Auntie Toa climbed out onto the perch with Ms. Whit's Daughter...from California, to see what was happening in The Great Backyard; however, there was no Great Backyard. There was only river. The Great Back Porch was partially underwater. Broken branches were blown everywhere. A small pine tree from places unknown had been uprooted and hurled onto the porch. Its ghostly roots bore witness to the awesome power of the wind.

The roof from the fishing dock was gone and the dock itself was covered by high water. A large wooden barrel had been swept down the river stopped only by the dock. Unable to go further, it spun around and around churning whatever contents lay inside.

Scattered everywhere were signs of the storm. A full sheet of plywood balanced precariously atop the branches of a tall pine tree.

No birds flew through the light gray sky.

"T'wind and d'rain have been playin' shenanigans again. It a'pears t'have had a whale of a time." Auntie Toa commented.

"Shore looks thet way t'me, Old Girl. This will take some time to pass. You and the young'un might ought to get as comfortable as ya kin. We're gonna be here fer a spell." Grander said.

"Everything is like...gone! Where is my Mother." Ms. Whit's Daughter...from California, uttered under her breath, staring at the total destruction around her.

They settled in to wait out the effects of the wind and the rain.

It took two days for the river to recede.

It was hard to say when morning came, but on that second day, the thick blanket of remaining clouds began to thin, allowing the sun to shine through the darkness. The wind blew but only as wind blows to move the clouds along. Water drops fell from everything. The Great Pine Trees washed clean by the storm stood as if untouched by the incredible force of the hurricane. That Big Old BullFrog croaked deep and low.

Birds flew through the air, calling to everyone that the storm was over. “Come out! Come out!”

Tutankhamen sat on the muddy riverbank watching the water flow down to the sea. The trio from the birdhouse hopped and climbed down the morning glory vines to join the others on the boardwalk. Slowly, everyone joined Tutankhamen.

Everyone except for Ms. Whit. Where was she? Where was Jeremiah? Ms. Whit’s Daughter ...from California, called to her mother. There was no answering call.

Soon everyone went looking for Ms. Whit. Grander went to see about the little frogs. Maybe Jeremiah had gone back to them.

There was no trail to follow. Not a clue to go by. No tracks. No spoor. Nothing. Evidence was washed out by the flooding waters of the West Pearl River.

Chapter Eleven
During the Storm

s. Whit held tightly to the narrow perch. The flash of light from the last terrible bolt of lightning gave her just enough time to see the general outlay of The Great Backyard. Thunder crashed and boomed, cracking the night with its deafening roar. She knew she could not hold on any longer.

Just believe...she heard the voice inside her say...just believe. Ms. Whit simply let go.

High above the second story of The Great House, Ms. Whit soared. Coming back to the edge of the river, she flew through the howling wind, first high then low, unable to control her direction, unable to see clearly. She held onto her tiny straw hat waiting for who knew what horrible end.

The terror she had feared was complete. More than anything, she wanted to imagine herself in a faraway land where only gentle breezes blew. Where rain fell lightly on warm soft leaves and storms stayed far away. But Jeremiah needed her. Somewhere deep inside she needed to find him, to learn whatever she was supposed to learn that would help her use her power. For now, her immediate problem was trying to avoid being smashed into a giant pine, or perhaps getting flattened against The Great House where Auntie Lo and Uncle Jackwere lived.

"This is it! This is it!" she yelled to herself. This is the end of the journey, ...dashed to bits, ...frog gone mad! Whatever made me think I could do this! Help! Heeeellllp! Somebody, help!"

The wind lifted her high above the house. She was being blown around in circles, first over the house then out to the fishing dock, back and forth over and over again. She realized she was in some huge churning whirlpool of wind. Incredibly, she began to get the hang of it. "Maybe...if...I...yeessss!!!! Yyyyiiiiipppppppeeee!"

The wind carried the sound of her joyful cry far away. No one heard her when the answer came. There was not another soul around to share in her triumph. Ms. Whit was flying. Maybe not the way she had hoped to fly, but she was in the air, directing her course and it was she who was in charge of her destiny.

She held on to the brim of her straw hat, using it as a rudder to steer in the direction of the wind. She soared over the trees, over the roof of The Great House, out to the fishing dock, across The Great Backyard and back again. This time she knew where she was going.

Each time the lightning flashed, she looked hard at the ground around her. She didn't see anything that might be Jeremiah. She would make one more pass over the area then head down river.

She heard the roof on the dock screech and moan. The force of the wind had been working the screws loose from the metal. She headed for the other side of the river, hoping to avoid any flying objects larger than herself, maybe even the roof from the fishing dock.

Sailing above the tin roof, a mighty flash of lightning split the sky.

Jeremiah! He was there on the roof hanging on with all his little might. Jeremiah J. L'Polo, soon to be crowned Prince, was about to be blown from the roof where only moments before the wind had snatched him from the river and thrown him atop the metal covering Uncle Jackwere used to shade his fishing dock.

Ms. Whit had only one thought. GET TO JEREMIAH! Instantly, she was beside him, hanging on for dear life as the wind howled around them.

The little prince-to-be smiled bravely. She tried to shout, to tell him to hold on to her. He only looked at her, he did not understand. They were both losing their grip. The wind whipped around them, pulling them from the dock.

Ms. Whit wasn't sure how she would take Jeremiah with her, but she was going to do everything in her power to see that it happened. She held herself tight against the roof and reached out to take Jeremiah's hand. This he understood and reached for her. The wind whipped his arm away, so she stretched her hand out farther still. Ms. Whit barely touched the tips of Jeremiah's fingers as the wind ripped and tore the roof screaming from the dock.

Holding on to Jeremiah with one hand, Ms. Whit squeezed his fingers and thought, Be safe.

Instantly, they were gone. The roof flew from the dock to be found at its new location a few miles down the river.

It had only taken a scant few seconds from the time Ms. Whit saw Jeremiah until they were flying high above the storm in the center of the hurricane's eye. Saysa Sweet Peaches came up beside them. She motioned for them to ride on her back. Understanding her gestures, Ms. Whit lit upon the HummingBunny's back with Jeremiah beside her.

Jeremiah was speechless. The wind was calm. The night sky was clear but for the stars and the moon. They were on the back of a creature he had never imagined or even dreamed of. He didn't know where they were going and he didn't care.

Saysa Sweet Peaches flitted along with the eye of the hurricane. Soon, another HummingBunny joined them. Then another and two more and another. Ms. Whit had wondered where HummingBunnies went during a storm.

The HummingBunny asked Ms. Whit if she would like to see a few sights until the storm passed over the parish. The little frog nodded her head, too tired to speak.

Saysa rose above the cushion of air they had been riding on and sped northwest. High over the brewing side of the hurricane into the cool night air. She flew many miles away from Louisiana, away from the storm. When daylight broke, they were flying along a tree line of tall pine trees. Ms. Whit didn't recognize the landscape. She didn't know they had reached the Rocky Mountains of Colorado. The home base of HummingBunnies.

Saysa Sweet Peaches headed straight to a tall thick pine tree and lit on one of its branches. Ms. Whit and Jeremiah hopped off the HummingBunny's back onto the thick limb of the tree. Saysa began to hum quite rapidly. Soon, several other HummingBunnies gathered around the travelers and greeted them warmly. Ms. Whit understood the humming language and translated to Jeremiah.

"They are honored to have the new Frog Prince come to visit," she said.

"The honor is mine," Jeremiah told her.

"You are wise to recognize this, little prince. You will be given the key to many doors now that your journey has begun. It is good that you have met the HummingBunnies. They will be an ally if you need them, and once you learn their language, they will teach you many things. Listen closely to what they have to say Jeremiah." Ms. Whit told him.

Saysa Sweet Peaches introduced Jeremiah to many families of HummingBunnies. Ms. Whit translated the humming.

He was dazzled by the newness of knowledge he was gaining. Never had he imagined such wonder. The "waiting pool" had not prepared him for this.

Jeremiah watched the HummingBunnies dance and flit through the branches of the tall pine trees. Their wings made a musical sound when they gathered together. It was a joyous sound, so sweet. Ms. Whit had not heard this music in a long time. She was happy to be sharing it with Jeremiah.

The HummingBunnies had a marvelous system of communicating and sharing in their community. Jeremiah paid close attention to the way it was organized. He may be able to use the knowledge one day, or so he thought. He sat on the tree limb for what seemed like hours, just listening to the magical music coming from the beating of the HummingBunny's wings.

Ms. Whit translated the song. It was a song for Saysa Sweet Peaches. Her mother sang it to her when she was a baby HummingBunny.

Sweet Little Baby

Fly on a soft wind below the clouds,
hovering,
listen to the warmth of sunshine,
Sweet little baby, kiss the petals of the honeysuckle vine.
Dance on the edge of moonglow
Spread your wings and fly!
Sweet little baby
Sweet Peachy baby
Spread your baby wings and fly!

Ms. Whit and Jeremiah were mesmerized. As evening fell the stars shone so brightly it seemed the light from their shine snuggled into the nooks and crevices of the pine tree like miniature Christmas lights. It was hard to remember it was storming at home. It was hard to think of anything but the wonderful place the HummingBunny had brought them to.

Ms. Whit had wished to be safe with the wee prince beside her. She couldn't imagine a safer, more beautiful place. She knew she needed to get home, to let everyone know they were safe. In the morning, she would ask Saysa Sweet Peaches which direction she needed to fly in.

When each little HummingBunny zipped away into the night, Ms. Whit and Jeremiah hopped onto a bough of pine to rest until daybreak. They would go home in the morning

Chapter Twelve
Axolotl

hen the sun rose, casting a warm glow across the valley, Saysa Sweet Peaches zoomed to the tree the frogs rested in. She had them hop onto her back again and flew off in search of breakfast.

Saysa Sweet Peaches dropped to the forest floor beside a beautiful mountain stream. She let the frogs off and landed on a patch of the grassy stream bed, her wings folding gently behind her. The frogs hopped about, happily catching insects, and making tiny splashes at the edge of the stream. Saysa Sweet Peaches flew off to a field of mountain wildflowers to eat the nectar from the blossoms.

Ms. Whit hopped onto a smooth river rock about a third of the way across the stream. She sat on the rock looking at the water in the stream. Jeremiah hopped over to join her, thoroughly enjoying himself.

"Jeremiah, look how clear TheWater is. See the fish. You can see things as if it were pure air. "

As they basked in the sun by the cold mountain stream, a flash of color zipped beneath the water and dove into the rocks on the other side of the stream. Ms. Whit looked to see if she could tell what it was. Deja vu. This had happened to her before. When she first met the HummingBunny. This wasn't a HummingBunny. She didn't know what it was.

As she stared at the spot the colorful fish disappeared into, Jeremiah hopped over next to her and asked, "What are you doing?"

"Searching." she replied.

"Searching for what?" he asked, puzzled.

"I saw a 'something'. I've never seen this 'something' before." She answered.

"Hmm. Can I help you find something?" he wanted to know.

"Sure. Come on over. Be still and watch the rocks." she instructed.

They sat together, staring at the bank of rocks. As they waited, Ms. Whit began to hum. It was a good tune, a song about Polka Dots and Moonbeams. They sat waiting. Waiting for the 'something', and humming.

Not two beats after she began to hum, a creature quite foreign to Ms. Whit poked its head out of the rocks. It was moving to the rhythm of the tune she was humming. Right behind the first fish was a second fish. Well, as she looked at them, she could see they were not fish at all. They had very long tails and a ring of spikes around their necks. Like a lion's mane, but with bright triangular spikes. One was bright pink and the other bright yellow. And they were dancing!

Ms. Whit stopped humming and tapped Jeremiah. He saw what she was up to and he stopped humming. The animals stopped dancing. They stood motionless on the floor of the cold mountain stream. They had four legs each and soft sweet faces. They had a dorsal fin that ran down the length of their backs starting behind their heads and ending at the tips of their tails.

The duet began again. The animals began to bob their heads to the rhythm. Ms. Whit and Jeremiah watched while the two animals swayed and wriggled to their voices.

The 'fish' Ms. Whit and Jeremiah found were salamanders. They are referred to as Axolotls. Axolotls' most favorite thing to do is dance. They dance in the cold clear mountain streams, creating a flurry of colorful trails. They are quick and graceful, making ripples in TheWater as they cavort and slide through the clear stream.

The frogs hummed and sang for a long time and it seemed the axolotls danced for just as long as the frogs would sing. Ms. Whit went through a variety of tunes she knew. She started out humming, but before long she was singing her entire repertoire. She sang out every song she could think of, which was about forty-leven songs altogether. The axolotls danced and the frogs sang.

The sun was warm when the HummingBunny landed beside the two little Frogs. She grinned at the sight of her friends from the river with her friends from the mountain stream. It was perfect.

Saysa Sweet Peaches knew the secret of the axolotls' dance. It was music. She had discovered it quite by accident, although she didn't know they could dance. There isn't a lot of music up where they live, except for birds and HummingBunnies. Of course, the wind makes music and TheWater is musical.

This particular day, however, Saysa Sweet Peaches was diving in the stream having a fabulous time preening and washing up in cold water. She was having such a good time she began to hum a song. As she sang, the axolotls came darting out from the rocks in all manner of dance, flitting, turning, spinning and doing pike dives to the tune of the HummingBunny's song. Saysa Sweet Peaches remembered it very well. It was definitely the highlight of the year.

Saysa lit beside the singing frog and hummed along with her friend to a tune she learned from Grander, Cattle Call. When it got to the part where the yodeling started, the axolotls swam to the surface of the water and yodeled.

As the Great Father MistleToad was hatched a hundred and forty-leven years ago it is true! The axolotls yodeled.

Saysa Sweet Peaches did not know they could yodel. It was wonderful. They stuck their little faces out of the water and yodeled. This was the definition of delight. Yodeling axolotls! It caused the HummingBunny to laugh. That caused the frogs to laugh. That was the second definition of delight.

Well now, time passes, and storms pass, and it gets to be late in the day, so you have to decide to sit still or get moving.

The two frogs hopped on the HummingBunny's back and waved good-bye to the axolotls. They shimmered in the water, still now, after the dance was finished., The frogs and the HummingBunny zoomed off, disappearing into the clear blue sky, heading south on a current of cool air.

It didn't take long to reach the West Pearl River. As I told you, HummingBunnies are very, very, very fast. She lit on the highest branch of the tallest pine tree, where her nest used to be. Saysa Sweet Peaches wondered where her nest had gone, but she was accustomed to losing homes, with the ones she built being so far up. It wouldn't take long to build another.

The trio looked around The Great Backyard and The Great House and The West Pearl River, everywhere the storm had left its mark. But the air smelled clean and fresh up in the top of the pine tree. The scent of honeysuckle wafting through the branches. Ms. Whit and Jeremiah sat on the branch where the nest used to be. She marveled at the view from the top. It was no wonder birds built their homes in trees. The view was breathtaking. As if to punctuate that thought, a flock of seagulls swept over the tree yelling for everyone to "Get up! Get up!"

Ms. Whit watched Jeremiah. He was experiencing so many things for the first time. She loved seeing the world through his eyes, imagining what it was like for him to see it from the top of the tallest pine tree overlooking his own backyard that ran down the banks of The West Pearl River.

Chapter Thirteen

How Jeremiah Saved Jasper

Daddy! Mother! Up here! Look up here!" Jeremiah called, nearly tumbling off the branch, in a free-fall to the muddy ground below. The search party could not hear him. He was much too far away. He saw them from the branch's edge. Everyone was gathering to compare notes and begin the search for Ms. Whit and Jeremiah all over again. They had been searching for hours, and though the storm had washed away any signs they may have left behind, they would not give up until all hope was lost. For now, hope was strong in their hearts, and they would keep looking until it was too dark to see.

Jeremiah leaned over the branch again, too excited to keep still. Ms. Whit pulled him back from the edge. Smiling warmly, she motioned for him to hop onto the HummingBunny's back.

"Hold on a bit Jeremiah, we'll fly down and meet them on the walkway," Ms. Whit told him. Jeremiah leaped upon the back of the softly reverberating creature as Ms. Whit climbed on board behind him. Saysa flitted and flew to the spot just above where the search party was gathering.

"Mother! Daddy! Here I am! Up here! Look up here!" he called.

The search party looked at each other. Where was the voice coming from?

"Did you hear that voice," Silky asked. "I hear him, I'm sure I hear Jeremiah mother. Don't you hear him, Grander?"

Jeremiah laughed aloud.

Saysa Sweet Peaches hovered over their heads. Ms. Whit smiled as the heads of the search party looked up into the sky. Saysa blocked the sun as she hovered. They couldn't see anything but an oddly shaped something with wings and a voice like Jeremiah 's. What had the storm done to him? Oh my, how different he had become.

Saysa zoomed from their spot to the top of the tallest pine tree and back in an instant. Bbbbbrrrreeetttt! Jeremiah, laughing and so happy to be home, waited for her to hover close to the ground then jumped from her back landing in front of his father.

"Our boy! Our boy is home." Jeremiah jumped into his father's arms.

Ms. Whit hopped from the HummingBunny's back, and Saysa Sweet Peaches simply disappeared. The searchers stared in wonder at the spot where Ms. Whit and Jeremiah had suddenly appeared. What mysterious creature had delivered The Prince and their beloved Ms. Whit back from the brink of the unknown? What had happened to them and how did they get back here? They all started talking at once, questioning the two little frogs to no end.

"My deah-ly b'loved we must give our de'ah ones a moment to catch a breath," Old Bully drawled. "My deah Ms. Whit, won't you tell us what great fortune has been b'stowed upon you and young Jeremiah that brings you back into the arms of yo b'loved family?"

She told them everything that had happened once she let go of the perch on the birdhouse nailed to The Great Back Porch, how she had found Jeremiah and where. She told them about the HummingBunny and the dancing salamanders. She didn't leave out any details except she had no idea how Jeremiah had wound up on the roof of the fishing dock.

Ms. Whit turned and asked Jeremiah, "How in the world did you come to be on the roof of Uncle Jackwere's fishing dock?"

"It was Jasper!" Jeremiah exclaimed.

"He saved me mama!" Jasper added, looking at his own mother.

"Yeah see, I saw Jasper being dragged by a fishing line that was tangled up on a limb. He was spinning around and around. We were watching stuff you never see in the water going straight down the river."

"Yeah, we did, we saw a bicycle and tow truck!" said Triple J

"Yeah, but when I saw Jasper, I just had ta' jump for him. I missed him, then I missed the fishing line and the hook too! The current was moving so fast we couldn't get to the riverbank, and then all of a sudden there was a huge tree trunk fell across the river just downstream a little ways from where we were and the tidal wave it caused lifted us right up from the water and set us on the tree trunk just like that!"

"What happened next Jeremiah, all we saw was your feet swimming after Jasper," said Finnian

"Then that alligator gar was swimming right after you. We thought you were goners for sure." said Willenor.

"I know! I know!" said Dancy and Tinga in unison.

"I don't know how, but the wind came along and scooped us both onto the riverbank. The fishing line was pulled clean off Jasper's leg and we just looked at each other, we were feelin' lucky. We weren't too far from the BackPipe, so we headed there." Jeremiah continued. "The last I saw of Jasper he was crawling over the edge of the pipe."

"That was the last I saw of you too Jeremiah." Jasper said.

"Cause about that time the biggest gust of wind I ever heard came howling like a racer over the Back Pipe, it felt like a hand picked me up and tossed me like a toy boat...seemed hours before Ms. Whit found me on the roof of that deck." Jeremiah concluded.

"I sure am glad you came after me," Jasper said, smiling sheepishly.

"Me too, cousin." Jeremiah grinned.

No one could say what force of nature put Jeremiah on the roof of the dock but get there he did. It was a good thing because if he hadn't been exactly where he was at the exact time he was there, then Ms. Whit wouldn't have seen him and there is absolutely no telling where this story would have ended.

Whether it was chance or some cosmic plan that made everything happen the way it happened, it was a lucky thing for Jeremiah that the river and the wind did what they did when they did it.

"Glory be and Saints of the Great Father MistleToady be praised!" declared Auntie Toa, who had fully recovered from her epic journey.

All over The Great Backyard were shouts of joy.

Everyone was cheering for Ms. Whit and Jeremiah and whatever strange creature had delivered them home.

Every frog, every turtle, every living thing that could was walking or hopping or crawling to where Ms. Whit sat with the other frogs.

The great feeling of joy spread to all the creatures living on the river. As the large group of small creatures gathered around, they talked and sang and told their stories about the hurricane. Some brought food and some played music, but they all shared in the goodness of being together.

Saysa Sweet Peaches was right. Ms. Whit could not save them all, they didn't all need saving, but because of her courage and belief in herself, she did save the one.

The Humans would be home soon. Jeremiah would be the Prince of Slidell soon, and Ms. Whit would be leaving The Great Back Porch and her beloved piano stool.

No one knew she was going. Not even Ms. Whit was certain, but there were a great many new adventures for her to go on and a great many new friends for her to meet. Tomorrow would be the third Saturday in June.

Tomorrow was the Coming Up of all Coming Ups, the crowning of the Prince of Frogs. It would prove to be a new beginning for some of those who lived on the banks of the West Pearl River

POLYVINYL CHLORIDE - PVC MADE IN USA

Chapter Fourteen
Cut to The Chase

Honk! Honk! Honk! Honk! Honk! The first pickup truck came bouncing over the gravel road. Honk! Honk! As the old vehicle came to a halt, many children and several adults came pouring over the sides of the bed carrying rakes and shovels and brooms and mops and buckets of old rags and toolboxes filled with hammers and nails, saws and screwdrivers, levels, string line and various other fixit gadgets.

Coming up behind the pickup were more cars filled with more children and more adults of various ages and abilities.

The word had spread quickly. Auntie Lo and Uncle Jackwere needed help.

The Great Backyard was in shambles. Boards were loose on the house. A window was broken. The dock that Uncle Jackwere built was missing a roof. There were broken limbs scattered across the yard and a full sheet of ply board still balanced on the upper branches of a tall pine tree.

There were people everywhere. Then, another pickup came down the gravel road loaded with ladders, and trash cans and coolers filled with sandwiches and more coolers filled with sodas and water and gallons of sweet tea and ice.

Did I say there were people everywhere? Oh yes, I did say that. Well, there were people everywhere. The entire neighborhood knew Uncle Jackwere and Auntie Lo were having a family reunion. Their guests would be arriving this very afternoon.

However, Auntie Lo and Uncle Jackwere hadn't known all these people were coming to help. The only one either one of them expected was Bro. Ron.

Auntie Lo had wanted everything to look nice for her company, but since the storm everything was topsy-turvy. She had decided to wait until after the weekend when everyone went home to do the major things. Except for the window. That would have to be replaced. The mosquitoes in Louisiana could be such a bother on a warm, wet summer night.

So, Auntie Lo called Kay-Kay to see if John could come help. Of course, John would be happy to lend a hand. And just as soon as Kay-Kay got off the phone with Auntie Lo she called Sara Katharine to ask if she could come. Then Kay-Kay called Ronny Sue who called Amy Elizabeth who called Virginia and Rebecca and Joanie who all called a friend.

Then Kay-Kay called her good friend Tom Selleck and he and all the other menfolk packed up their tools and here everyone was in about an hour, ready to help Auntie Lo and Uncle Jackwere.

They all shook hands and compared damages and hugged the womenfolk. The men patted the young ones on their heads and the younger ones wrapped themselves around their mother's legs and peeked from behind them or buried their shy little heads into a shoulder only to poke a nose out later on.

Everyone got busy right away. Even the children could be a big help. They picked up tons of pine cones and tree limbs and various bits of debris, some of it recognizable, and some of it pieces of unknown origin.

Three of the adult men and one of the women put a new roof on the dock that Uncle Jackwere built. The missing boards were replaced, the loose boards on the house were tightened, touch up paint was applied, somebody went to the store for wood. The big house was looking good as new.

The statues around the fishless pond were righted. The mud washed from the house, the walkways, the dock and the little rowboat. Miraculously, the rowboat was still tied to the dock, though it had to be fished from the water. After which, it was washed and now sat bobbing gently with the current of the river. Somebody else went to the store for a new saw blade.

The Humans worked hard at getting everything back to where it belonged. They were nearly done. All that was left was getting the sheet of plywood down from the big tree.

The men gathered around the tree to have a look at the situation. The ladies, knowing how long the men could be, started getting things ready for lunch. Somebody went to the store for pickles.

Uncle Jackwere's son and Danny's father were going to do the job of getting the plywood down "in a jiffy," one of them had said, ...or had they agreed?

Big Dan tied a rope around his chest, then coiled another rope and carried it up to use for lowering the plywood. He climbed the ladder and crawled out onto the limb where the plywood rested.

"Make sure you got plenty of rope,"' Harvey called up to the two men.

Uncle Jackwere's son John climbed up after Big Dan.

It wasn't long before everyone began to gather around the tree keeping a safe distance just in case the plywood became airborne, or any tree branches fell from the trees or one of the men came tumbling to the ground. No one wanted to see that happen. But if anything did happen, not one boy there wanted to miss it. You couldn't be too careful in a situation like this.

After examining the stability of the plywood, Big Dan crawled out onto the center of the wood discovering a large knot hole about a third of the way from the end. This discovery would make the job much easier than he had anticipated.

Taking the opposite end of the rope from the one tied around his chest, Big Dan tied it on to what looked to be a sturdy branch above his head. That would be his security rope. Using one end of the second rope, he began threading it through the knot hole.

In the distance, they all heard Mr. Hawthorne's big English Mastiff, Daphne, barking cheerfully. It seemed the echo crossed the river a couple of times then bounced off the trees in The Great Backyard.

Big Dan looked towards the sound then back to the task at hand.

The Humans standing around the tree were talking and watching the men. Some were calling suggestions up to them. Big Dan grinned when Harvey Slater pointed out the possibility of Big Dan sitting on the plywood and sailing it down to the ground. When the chuckles died down, they heard Daphne again. She was getting closer.

Big Dan was tying off the knot when around the corner of the big house came Mr. Hawthorne's dog.

She was in hot pursuit of Robin, Auntie Lo's favorite cat.

It happened so fast no one agreed on what came first. They did agree on one point, Big Dan and John were two lucky people.

Now, Daphne wouldn't hurt Robin. She only wanted to play with the cat. Daphne had been cooped up in a hotel room for the better part of six days and wasn't thrilled with being inside. She just wanted to play with somebody...anybody. She'd been to the river and hadn't found a single turtle. All the children that were left in the neighborhood were at Auntie Lo and Uncle Jackwere's. There wasn't anyone else to chase, no one to throw sticks for her to fetch, so quite naturally, Daphne went looking for a playmate.

Needless to say, when Robin the cat saw the enormous dog come charging through the front yard, she did what any self-respecting cat would do. She stood up, her fur bristling, her back arched, then as Daphne came closer, Robin jumped a good four and a half feet straight up in the air. She hit the ground hissing and spewing then took off like a shot in the opposite direction of the huge English Mastiff. If cats get goose bumps, you can bet Robin had them. Her fur stood straight on end, her tail bushed out like a feather duster.

Robin wanted safety. Daphne wanted to play. It seemed to the enormous dog that she had found a willing partner and that the cat had caught on rather quickly. Daphne was the chaser. Robin was the chasee. It was the oldest game around and that is how it is played.

Across the yard came the howling cat with the huge dog barking joyously at her heels.

Robin made a beeline straight through the crowd of people and up the tall pine tree in four seconds flat. (some say it was eight while others would make a bet on three). The cat climbed on the branch directly above the plywood while Big Dan balanced on the end of the wooden sheet.

Robin looked down from the limb, her eyes wide with fright.

In the meantime, Daphne had tried to climb the ladder John was standing on. Although she couldn't do much more than put her paws on a middle rung, when she pushed off, the ladder came with her and so did John.

"Whoa! Whoa! Whoa! Somebody grab that hound!" he yelled.

John grabbed for the branch above his head as the ladder swayed far from the tree. John's toes barely touched the top rung. He tried to hold on, but the ladder slipped away from his feet.

"Get the ladder! Get the ladder," someone shouted.

"Here kitty-kitty." Big Dan called gently to the poor terrified cat. She ignored him, her eyes were shut now. The plywood swayed far to the left.

"I…can't...hold...on...much...longer," John croaked, his teeth clenched tightly. He was right. The ladder fell into a large flowering bush, leaving John hugging the branch with all four limbs. He hung from the tree twenty feet from the ground.

"Get...the...ladder...somebody!"

John was slowly slipping from the thick, rough branch.

"Here kitty-kitty, here kitty-kitty." Dan called soothingly to the big cat.

Big Dan gritted his teeth trying hard to keep his voice calm. Robin opened her eyes to a narrow slit and looked at the man balancing on the plywood. One hand reached for the cat while the other stretched far behind, helping him keep his balance on the wood. Big Dan looked like he was surfing through the tall pine tree.

"Hold on John! Hold on!"

The men raised the ladder beneath John's feet.

"Can you drop down to the top rung man? Steady now. Steady John." someone directed him.

It was a good thing John was in such excellent condition. He lowered his feet to the top rung of the tall ladder while four men below held it steady. He stood on the top step of the ladder and raised himself onto the limb he'd been clinging to. Then he took a seat on it, ready to assist Big Dan if he needed it.

Daphne started barking again. Mr. Hawthorne grabbed her collar and gave the command to sit, then another to be silent.

She looked up at her Master, her eyes laughing with all the fun she was having.

"Me did good hunh, me made chase, me did good,." she seemed to be saying.

She licked Mr. Hawthorne's hand and sat by his side panting and laughing, dripping smelly river water from her sleek dappled coat.

While Robin's attention was temporarily diverted as she looked down at the pea sized dog that only moments before had seemed such a huge menace, Big Dan decided this was the time to make his move.

He grabbed for the cat, the cat grabbed for Big Dan, the plywood slid several inches across the branches, dipped slightly, the rope slid from the knot hole, then the board settled again. The crowd below gasped then fell silent. Everyone watched the plywood, waiting with bated breath to see what would happen next.

As Big Dan continued his balancing act, the cat jumped onto his head, her tail in his eyes. She sat with her claws hooked into his shirt collar, her hind legs on either side of his face. She was too scared to move.

"Nice kitty...nice kitty," Big Dan called to her gently.

He tried to blow her tail out of his face so he could see where he stood. Robin only growled low and twitched her tail. She wasn't about to move. Carefully and slowly, Big Dan reached up to grab her from his head. The slight movement of his arms unbalanced the plywood and it shifted again.

Someone below shouted, "Look out Dan, that plywood is comin' down!"

As if in slow motion, the wooden sheet began to slide across the branches. Big Dan felt it move under his feet. There wasn't time to think of a plan. Big Dan had to act right then. He lunged for the rope tied to the tree. When he did, Robin jumped off his head onto the plywood. It was just enough of a push to get the sheet airborne. The crowd below scattered in all directions as the board came sailing to the ground.

The cushion of air beneath the heavy sheet of wood allowed for a surprisingly soft landing. The plywood tipped once then glided gently to the earth. When it touched the ground, Robin looked around. The first person she saw was Auntie Lo. The cat meowed then stepped off the board. Auntie Lo picked her up, speaking to her in gentle tones of reassurance.

When the plywood sailed out of the tree, Big Dan grabbed wildly for the end of the rope still tied to the limb. Desperate to keep his balance, he appeared to be running in place for a few seconds. His arms rotating wildly, Big Dan yelled something no one had ever heard before. He spun around and, in slow motion, Big Dan sailed over the large tree limb taking a nosedive out of the tree.

He yelled again, another phrase no one had ever heard before, and flipped head over heels, landing solidly astride the limb below the one he had just been standing on. Thump! Big Dan hit the limb. A thin fracture in the limb cracked and broke away. He was stuck on a small stub of the large limb hugging the trunk of the tree. Pale and holding his breath.

Every man below witnessed the entire scene from the safety of the ground. John wasn't far from the man when he met the immovable tree limb. Every man jack of them cringed and looked away. When they looked back, Big Dan had a strained look on his face.

"Dan, you alright man?" John asked in sympathy.

"I think so." he answered squeakily.

"Hold on just a little while longer, I'll climb around and help you down."

John swung his leg over the branch. He stood up and climbed through the branches until he was directly above Big Dan.

One of the men below picked up the end of a rope that had fallen to the ground. The other end was still attached to Big Dan.

"Can you throw it up here to me?" John called down to the man with the rope.

"I dunno John, seems like mebbe I'd knock him out'a the tree. Mebbe somebody oughta bring it up to you."

Danny and the other grandchildren had been watching this unusual undertaking since Robin had scaled the giant pine tree. Like everyone else, Danny wanted to help. He surveyed the situation and found an opportunity where he might do just that.

"Dad?" Danny called up to Big Dan.

"Yeah son," Big Dan answered.

"Dad, you know the bow and arrows you got me last week?"

"Yeah, Danny, what are you thinking?" Big Dan asked.

"I'm thinking there will be fewer birds around here." Uncle Jackwere mumbled under his breath.

"I've been practicing Dad. I think I can tie this end of the rope to one of my arrows and shoot it right up over the branch above you. When it falls, the guys down here can lead the rope out until it's tight enough to raise you off the limb. Then John can direct you away from the tree while the guys lower you down to the ladder," Danny suggested hopefully. Think that would be a good idea Dad?" Danny sounded hopeful.

John grinned. So did Big Dan. They both thought it would be an excellent idea.

"Danny, listen to me son, you'll have to aim the arrow higher than what it looks like you'll need to, O.K.?"

"John can get it in position from up here. Oh, and Danny?"

"Yeah, Dad?"

"Son, I know you can do it." Danny and Jake tied the end of the rope to the end of the arrow. Almost everyone had to make sure it was tight enough. Finally, Danny was ready. He backed up from the tree until he could look up into the branches and see the very spot he wanted to send the arrow. He knew he would have to pull the string tight and hold the arrow as straight as possible. He had to compensate for the added weight and the drag of the rope. He looked down the shaft, aimed the tip of the arrow just above the branch where the rope should go, took a deep breath, let it out slowly, then pulled the string back as far as he could and let the arrow fly.

Swoosh! Off it went, true to the aim Danny took. It sailed over the branch, cutting through the air with the sound of perfect direction. It was an easy shot for Danny, but more than that, it was an important shot. He liked being known for a good thing. It was so much better than getting into trouble or being too hard headed to see he could do something good with his talent.

Uncle Jackwere was right. Danny was a very good shot.

The entire group of Humans cheered. The men tousled Danny's hair and patted his shoulder. Danny grinned from ear to ear. This was a lot better than empty bird nests.

John caught the rope and leaned against the trunk of the tree while untying the arrow. Throwing the rope over the branch above, John let the end drop over the limb. He held on to the overhead limb while the men below caught the rope and began to walk it out. Big Dan was still astride the large tree limb, facing the trunk.

"Alright Danny Boy, we're ready to pull you up off that limb, you ready?" Harve called up to the stranded man.

"Good and ready Harve, I'm coming down boys...hold tight to that rope."

"Let's pull 'im up boys," Harve said. The men below pulled on the rope, lifting Dan from the limb. John guided the rope towards the ladder and as Big Dan's feet touched it, the Humans below released a collective breath they were holding. Slowly, Big Dan stepped down the ladder one rung at a time. Easy and steady, he came to the bottom rung. He stepped off and John stepped on. He climbed down quickly as he'd had much practice with ladders and ropes. John and Big Dan were both firefighters.

With both men safely on the ground, the crowd erupted in cheers. Oscar Woodward brought out his big Swiss Army knife and cut the rope from Big Dan's chest. The man would be bruised and sore for several days, but all in all he walked away with only a few scratches and a lot of cat hair, mostly up his nose.

"Looks like ya had plenty a' rope," Harvey said as he shook Big Dan's hand and grinned.

"I'd say we had enough Harve, and thanks." Big Dan said sincerely.

"Don't mention it Dan." Harvey replied.

"Good job boys." Judge Snikeris congratulated the men on a job well done.

The Judge and about fifteen others crowded around the two men, making jokes and discussing the newly developed fine art of tree surfing and riding on a flying plyboard.

Danny waited for his father. When Big Dan could finally get away from the guys, he went to his son.

"That was a fine shot son, first time, clear and true. I'm very glad you came up with the idea. There is no telling how long I might have been stuck up in that tree."

Big Dan put his arm around Danny's shoulder.

"That's O.K. Dad, I'm glad I was here too. And hey Dad, I think I do want to join that archery club, that be O.K.?"

"That would be most O.K. son."

Danny grinned. After all the whoops and hollers everyone had given him after such an easy shot, maybe a little competition with the other kids would be a lot of fun.

Jake came up to Danny as he stood beside his father. The boys hadn't said much about the bird nest incident. It was kind of understood after Danny's father spoke to him about it. Uncle Jackwere really didn't have much use for slingshots and such, but he knew Danny had a talent that would be wasted if not redirected to something positive. Jake had his hands in his pockets waiting for the other boy.

"I'll see ya Dad. Jake and me are gonna go to the dock."

"Wait Danny. I was thinking maybe you could show me how to use the bow and arrows. We could set up some targets and practice for a while, that is, if you want to."

Jake saw Danny's smile and knew his friend understood what the request meant. He accepted something they'd been at odds over.

"Sure Jake, I'll show you how to shoot arrows. It's easy, see, all you gotta do is see the arrow hit the target."

The boys went to set up a firing range and, as they found the articles needed to practice, a crowd of other kids joined them. They brought out slingshots and BB guns and two other kids had run home to get their own bows and arrows.

There was a real competition gearing up and plenty of crack shot adults who would oversee the games.

"Company's coming," someone hollered to Auntie Lo.

Gravel crunched under the tires of the cars coming down the road. Several more children and several more adults came pouring out of the cars. Did I say there were people everywhere?

From out of the woodwork came tables and chairs and more food and more people. There were nearly a hundred and forty-leven humans out in The Great Backyard. People gathered to lend a hand and to celebrate family.

It was time to eat.

Uncle Jackwere had something to say. He'd been thinking about it all morning. He felt like the richest man in all the parish. He'd watched his community give him and his lovely bride back their home. They would gather at other homes in the days to come to help others get back home too. This was what made his house a home, his community one to be proud of.

Uncle Jackwere wasn't keen on giving speeches, but with so many people gathered around, it was the perfect time to tell them what was on his mind. So, he asked for everyone to listen up for a minute, he had a couple of things to say.

"Speech," someone hollered. "Speech!"

"No, not a speech," Uncle Jackwere said as he walked to where his bride of fifty-six years sat at the end of the table.

"You all know I am not a man of many words."

Everyone laughed. They all knew he was a man of very many words. Carefully chosen, so positive and uplifting, filled with the spirit of love he felt for his family and his friends.

"Lemme tell you all a little something about this fella I heard about in Saudi Arabia, he had a oil company and made so much money he couldn't spend it in a hundred lifetimes. Imagine? I heard about another fella in Texas had so many cattle he couldn't count them all in one day and his ranch was so big he couldn't get across it in less than three days on horseback. Then there was a man in Africa who bought a diamond mine just so he could give his wife as many diamonds as she wanted. I've heard hundreds of stories about men who made fortunes and had so much wealth they could never want for anything. Everything they ever needed or desired was at their fingertips. I don't envy those men. I wouldn't trade one day of living with this beautiful woman right here for every fortune ever made. I wouldn't trade one memory with any one of you for any treasure they could ever offer. See, to me I am the richest man I ever heard about...and all the jewels that ever hung from any crown are right here with Lo and me. Thank you all for giving me my fortune. For the blessings you are to us. We thank God for you every day."

Looking at the crowd gathered around him, Uncle Jackwere smiled.

"Now before this becomes a starving mob, would someone please pass the biscuits and get Betty a tissue while you're at it. I think she is going to get emotional on us again."

One by one and several at a time, the Humans started clapping. Someone stood up then somebody else followed suit. Soon everyone was standing, they whistled and hollered at Uncle Jackewere.

He raised his hands for them to settle down and called on Reverend R. Mullen to give thanks for their health and for all the delicious food they were about to enjoy.

Lily, who was then only three and a half years old, came walking towards Uncle Jackwere, a huge platter of biscuits in her small hands.

"Me bwing you da bissiks Unca' Jackwuh," she innocently said and smiled up at him adoringly.

Uncle Jackwere took the dish from her tiny hands. "Thank you honey."

Uncle Jackwere picked the little girl up and sat her on his knee. He kissed the top of her head and buttered her biscuit. Uncle Jackwere knew that no treasure on Earth was worth one minute of this day. And not all the tea in London could buy a moment of true friendship or the heart of a loving family. Uncle Jackwere was a grateful, happy man.

Chapter Fifteen
The Coming Up

Ms. Whit looked down through the branches of the tall tree across the river from Flatter Rock. There was a lovely view from where she sat. The decorating committee had outdone themselves. There were flowers everywhere. They were looped across the elephant ears, hanging from the edge of the rock over the river, wrapped around the cattails and strewn across the big rock, it hung from the moss on the trees beside the riverbank.

Pink flowers from the fields behind the neighbor's barn and dark red periwinkles from the beds that lined the boardwalk had been placed beautifully along the pathway to Flatter Rock. Delicate pearly white water lilies encircled the stone platform. Garlands of greenery adorned the banks of the West Pearl River. There were purple winecups, pink and yellow lantana flowers, yellow esperanza, huge lavender morning glories and pink primroses scattered randomly about the stage that would soon welcome the new frogs and crown the young Prince.

Ms. Whit sighed. Things had changed, she felt it. Everything around her seemed fresher and newer and yet the same somehow. Maybe it was just the storm that had washed everything anew. Whatever it was, she was sure she was going to be busy doing new things, meeting new friends, seeing new places she couldn't even imagine yet. She was ready. She had found what she had come to The Great Back Porch to find. She learned the greatest lesson Ms. Whit could ever learn, to her there is no such thing as peace and quiet!

Now it was time for her to move on. Things had changed and Ms. Whit had changed too. She wanted to meet new friends. Friends like the HummingBunny and the dancing axolotls. She was amazed at every new turn. The world was unfolding, yielding to her the joy and the gifts of living on a planet that welcomed life.

She was so proud of Jeremiah. He and the rest of the upcoming frogs were getting ready for the big event. Creatures of every description were gathering at Flatter Rock to witness the crowning of the new Prince and to welcome the newest members of the community into their families. The great cycle of all living things continued and from this day forward, Jeremiah, along with help from his Elder Frogs, would lead them through whatever adventures came their way.

That Big Old BullFrog Travis croaked deep and low...jug-o-rum...jug-o-rum...jug-o-rum. Frogs began hopping in from all over the river bank up and down. It was quarter past noon on Saturday. How the frog's knew it was anybody's guess, but punctual they were.

Soon, Flatter Rock was covered with frogs and every other kind of creature that came to celebrate the Coming Up.

That Big Old BullFrog sat at the edge of the rock looking out over the river. He slowly turned to face the congregation then raised his warty old, webbed hands.

"Mah deahly b'loved, hon'ored guests and good friends, it is indeed a great hon'ah to have you all heah on this most auspicious o'cassion. We ah gath'uhed heah to welcome our young ones to the banks. Up from TheWatah' they will come to be paht of our commun'ity. T'learn and t'serve and t'be a part of somethin' much greater than themselves. This new generation will be our lea'dahs one day. What we teach and entrust to them, they will pass to the next gen'a' ration. Let us be stalwart in all we do. They hold us in the palms of their ver'ah hands."

Frogs were restless and birds were calling, rabbits jumped about the big rock while raccoons eyed the piles of food. Mice and water rats scampered about the goings on in anticipation of the celebration. Jeremiah's mother gave them all a stern look and they all settled down to wait out the spoken portion of the celebration. Wanting only to partake of the delicious delectables.

"Dear ones, it is my priv'ledge to intro'duce to you the newest mem'bas of our family." The Old Bullfrog smiled hugely.

The little ones had been waiting under the overhang of Flatter Rock, hardly able to keep from hopping about the great rock. Tutankhamen had been having a tough time keeping them quiet until That Big Old BullFrog Travis gave the signal for the first little Frog to make an appearance.

That Big Old BullFrog called out the first name.

"Jasper Jedidiah Jenkins." The BullFrog spoke clearly. "Welcome home Jasper."

Triple J., his cousins called him. Jasper hopped onto the rock, sort of a 'rock hop' if you will. He bowed low to That Big Old BullFrog amid cheers and applause from everyone there. Jasper joined his family to wait for the others to come ashore.

"Hoppy Soo Ling."' The Big BullFrog called the next one up. "Welcome home Hoppy Soo."

Hoppy Soo was a tiny little froglette. She is oh so shy and blushed when The BullFrog patted her on the head. Hoppy Soo joined her mother and father, Tinga and Ching Da.

"Dancy D'Ette Longspur." The BullFrog continued. "Welcome home Dancy D."

The BullFrog watched the little frog everyone called Dancy D hop onto the rock. She danced across the rock to join her family. Dancy D got her name for how she loved to dance across the lily pads.

"Hector De La Cruz Montoya Jr." The BullFrog continued. "Welcome home Heck."

That Big Old BullFrog shook hands with the little Frog who hopped beside him on the rock.

Heck's mother was crying when he came up from the river. He was their first son. Their family was almost as large as the Wickershams' clan of seventeen children. The Montoya's having only fourteen, all of them girls besides Heck. But Mrs. Montoya cried each time one of her children came up from TheWater. She was happy to see them.

"Finnian Chauncey McRoadie,." the Old BullFrog called. "Welcome home Finny."

Finnian was Auntie Toa's great-great-great-grandson. He was the fourth generation of McRoadies to be hatched on the West Pearl River. He had a strong character and was a most handsome lad.

"Cassiopia MorningGlory Vivareaux," That Old BullFrog pronounced, reaching for the little frog's hand.

"Welcome home Cassie de'ah."

Cassie was Ms. Whit's great aunt Agnes' third cousin on her mother's side, once removed. Cassie had Ms. Whit's love for music and would sing at the drop of a June bug.

"Wigintin Cedric Wickersham." That Old BullFrog smiled broadly at Wiggy's perseverance. "Welcome home Wiggy."

Wiggy was the runt, but he had spirit. He had to try three times before he made it to the top of the rock. Wiggy would not stop trying. A huge grin spread across his small face while the congregation cheered him on.

"Willenor Fredrica Delahunty." That Old BullFrog bowed low to the little Frog. "Welcome home Willeno'oh."

Willenor wanted to be called by her given name, Willenor. She wasn't one for nicknames, although that was fine for the others. Calling her Willy or Freddy just would not do. Willenor was the brightest, smartest frog anyone had ever known. She was always thinking, always wondering about the oddest things. She wanted to know everything she could about everything that was.

Willenor was the last frog to hop onto the rock. She stretched her legs as far as she could and kissed That Old BullFrog on his warty cheek. The Old BullFrog smiled at the little girl frog and patted her smooth wet head.

All the little frogs gathered around the Old BullFrog.

"To Family," he said. "Welcome one and all to yo'ah new home."

Each of the little ones was welcomed. It didn't matter if they were short or tall. It made no difference if they were large or small. They were all welcomed. Each welcomed. Their differences were an asset to the community. Each talent and each gift a blessing to everyone else.

There was a loud thumping of feet and flapping of wings. A raucous call went out from the flock of seagulls. Buzzing and trilling, hoots and hollers, whoops and yells, shouts and tingling bells all sounded to welcome the new frogs to the family. Oh, but it was a glorious sight.

Ms. Whit's Daughter...from California, was so excited she hopped over to the young ones and started singing a song. The backup group was already there and Chat was ready for the Coronation number, but this was indeed a surprise. No one knew Ms. Whit's Daughter...from California, even knew how to sing! She stepped up beside That Big Old BullFrog Travis and together they sang a song. The Valley Girl and the Baritone. Who knew!

Here Come the Little Ones

Here they come,
Big and little ones,
They come in dancing on a dream,
High hopes sliding down a moonbeam,
Smiling, loving, bring a little sunshine,
Oh they touch this heart of mine,
They are Joy
They are Love
They are Hope
Here they come!
Here they come!
Here come The Little Ones!
Oh, the little ones!
Deep in our hearts the little ones come
A kiss, a hug, cute as a June bug!
Take my hand, we'll go for a ride
I'll be like a shadow by your side!
The sky is the limit
The world is a clam
Wherever you go that's where I am
For you are the Love
The Hope
And the Joy that comes
on heavenly wings,
angels always sing to
The Little Ones!
They bring a little sunshine
And melt this heart of mine
They are Joy
They are Love
They are Hope
Glory days!
Here they come!
Here come The Little Ones!
Oh listen to the song
Here come The Little Ones,
The Little Ones Come,
The Little Ones Come!

Oh my, how the frogs shouted for joy. How they danced and hopped about. How lovely was this day! Welcoming the new members was just the way every baby anything should be welcomed into the world.

Across the river, Jeremiah was waiting. He sat on Tutankhamen's broad back listening to the joyful sounds of welcome from the many different creatures gathered at the great rock. Jeremiah was happy for them. He had made life-long friends with each of them and would do his very best to serve them well.

Suddenly, a hush fell over the river. That Big Old BullFrog Travis gave a signal to Chat, who was standing on a wooden crate left by the storm. It was time for the Coronation to begin.

Lord Chatterly lifted his flute. He looked about for Ms. Whit. He hadn't seen her all morning. Well, he couldn't wait any longer. Chat started to play the music he had rehearsed for the coronation. From the top of the tall pine tree came the clear sweet voice of the frog who had learned to use her Imagination. She could fly. She could do anything she set her mind to do. Everyone held a single breath as the song came pouring out of the top of the tall pine tree. It was Ms. Whit's special song for the new Prince. Her gift to Jeremiah.

My Prince

Oh my Prince,
Your spirit comes from long ago and far away,
For you to learn and as you grow to teach our ancient ways,
One mark was put upon your shining face,
The kiss of Fate, one kiss from Fate.
My Prince, be strong, let your wisdom guide you,
My Prince, be brave, count on the courage there inside you,
My Prince, be kind, help each little one around you,
And oh my Prince remember this,
Love each of those who will surround you.
For when you lead there must be one who follows,
And when you teach there must be one who's learning,
Then when you reach for dreams, for all that you can be,
Then oh my Prince remember this, reach high and just believe.
Look inside,
Don't be afraid for you will stumble as you go along your way
Look up high,
There's always something more to keep you humble on your way,
No, don't be afraid...you'll never be alone upon your way,
And oh my Prince remember this,
There is love upon your way.
Oh my Prince, be strong, let your wisdom guide you
Oh my Prince, be brave, count on the courage there inside you
Oh my Prince, be kind, help each little one around you,
And oh my Prince remember this
Love each of those who will surround you.
Oh my Prince...believe,
Oh my Prince...believe,
Oh my Prince...believe...just believe.

Not one sound, not even crickets, nothing but Ms. Whit and Lord Chatterly's music pierced the air. Until the last verse, Ms. Whit had stayed perched on the pine branch. As she ended the song, she appeared beside Jeremiah on Tutankhamen's wide green back. She reached for him, wrapping her arms around the little Prince to be. He hugged her back, not wanting to let go.

That Big Old BullFrog Travis saw her nod to him. It was time for everyone to meet Jeremiah. He hoped his speech would be remembered for as long as her song would be. He looked around the great circle and knew they had all felt the love and devotion of the beautiful song Ms. Whit had sung to Jeremiah.

Jeremiah jumped from Tutankhamen's broad green back, landing beside the Old BullFrog. Miss Silky and her parents beamed with pride.

"That's our boy! That's our boy!" Jeremiah's father could not be contained. He was so excited he jumped on his one good leg.

The Big Old BullFrog held up his warty old gnarly webbed hands.

"May Ah have yo'ah un'divided atten'shun please. Ahem, ...frogs and de'ah friends. We have come ta'getha' to witness a most unusual and highly uncommon affair. The crowning of the Prince of Frogs. We have fo' time untold been searchin' for ou'ah new Prince. One who could take the place of ou'ah be'lov'ed Prince Zardiack, who was captured by a ruthless band of ma'rauding pirates many years ago. It has taken ou'ah devoted Inspect'ah Mortimer McGillacuddy a ve'rah long time to find the hatchlin' that fits the description in the legend of the Prince of Slidell. He has been found de'ah ones. Found with the perfect mark. The Kiss of Fate."

"Finnian, will you please come forward," asked That Old BullFrog. Finnian brought a crown and presented it to That Big Old BullFrog. Jasper followed with a scepter made from a pine stick.

Hoppy Soo Ling presented the Old BullFrog with a robe fashioned from the softest leaves from The Great Backyard.

"Jeremiah J. L'Polo, you have been chosen as the next Prince of Slidell. The mark upon yo'ah young brow has been revealed and you have been tried by wa'tah and wind. Yo'ah time has come to be lead-ah.

If you choose to accept the responsibility, you must protect the young, hon'ah the ElderFrogs, and treat all livin' creatures with respect. I am asking these things in truth, what say you?"

Nobody breathed. This was the one and only chance Jeremiah had to refuse to become the Prince of Slidell. No one had ever been forced to take reign. And nobody would blame him if he refused. Being the Prince of Frogs would not be easy. He would be held up as an example for all Frogdom. Everything he said would be heard. Everything he did would be watched. Everything he came to believe would become a part of his legacy.

Jeremiah never batted an eye. He knew for a long time what his destiny would be. What he would do. Where he was going. The direction he wanted to take. But Jeremiah liked a little drama too.

"With all due respect ...and after long consideration and careful thought into everything you have presented to me today my dear Old Bully, my fellow frogs and friends, I find I simply, well, in order to keep a clear conscience-," Jeremiah paused for a good eight seconds as he looked at the crowd., Everyone leaned in closer to hear. Then he looked back at the Old BullFrog.

"I find I simply cannot..."

The crowd gasped.

"I find I cannot say no, I accept the reign as the Prince of Slidell with honor, and I hereby promise to keep the traditions and ancient ways of Frogs forever. I will protect the little ones, honor the ElderFrogs, and treat all living creatures with honor and respect."

There was a collective sigh of relief, but the Old BullFrog wasn't done yet. They all knew it.

"Then by the power vested in me by the Great Father MistleToad, I crown you The Prince of Frogs. My fellow frogs and friends, I present to you Jeremiah Jeffrey L'Polo, the forty-twelfth Prince of Frogs."

The Old BullFrog placed the robe around Jeremiah's shoulders, the crown upon his head, then handed him the scepter.

"Prince Jeremiah, m'boy, you may co'mence to bein' the Prince of Slidell," The Old BullFrog proclaimed, finishing his duties.

"YeeeeeeeeHaaaaaaaa!" yelled Grander, throwing his hat into the air.

That was all it took. There was absolute and utter chaos on the rock. It was clearly a case of joyful pandemonium. Frogs were leaping and jumping. The Escargot danced. The Lady Bugs jittered. Dragonflies hovered low over the revelers and huge flocks of birds flapped their wings in jubilation. Feet were thumping loudly as Chat trilled his flute, and though the new Prince didn't have dominion over anyone but frogs, all creatures love a good Coronation.

The Coming Up lasted until the wee hours of the morning. Guests from many far-a way places came to pay their respects and to celebrate. Jeremiah greeted two hundred and sixty-nine Frogs, seventy eight racoons, sixteen alligators, seventeen armadillos, eighteen possums, nineteen lizards, twelve salamanders, seven schools of fish, twenty four dragonflies, seven toads, four cats, two dogs, and the partridge from the peach tree, not to mention all the other birds of a feather, including Hannah the Great Heron who was none other than the Express Service Grander and Ms. Whit's Daughter...from California, had taken to get to Flatter Rock. He met heads of State and Royalty, he danced with so many little froglettes and other little girl creatures he had blisters on his toes for days.

Everyone had a splendid time.

Then sometime later, though I'm not exactly sure how long, after everyone had eaten and sang and danced and played so many delightful games and after the last lightning bug flew into the brushy undergrowth across the river, Ms. Whit sat on Flatter Rock enjoying the company of the last few guests of the very last Coming Up she would be attending on Flatter Rock.

The Costume Party
Deb Mus

Chapter Sixteen

Sometimes the End is a New Beginning

Ms. Whit, Ms. Whit's Daughter...from California, That Big Old BullFrog Travis, Grander, Lord Chatterly and the new Prince of Slidell sat upon Flatter Rock watching the last few straggler stars wink dimly in the early morning sky. Frog Songs sounded clear and sweet across the river up and down. It was cool and pleasant as the council of assorted creatures talked about the great success of the Coming Up and the plans they had for the near future.

Grander and Ms. Whit's Daughter...from California, would be taking The Express back to Choke Canyon in a few days. Grander had big plans for the winter. There was a huge celebration still in the planning stages being held in McMullen County back in Texas. Springtime would be a great time for a horned toad drive. Grander was looking forward to the drive. The Cowboys of Calliham would ride again.

That Big Old BullFrog Travis was already living his adventure right here on the banks of the West Pearl River. He had no desire for traveling to far-away places. He was happy to already be home where he was needed for the next generation of frogs.

Lord Chatterly would remain with Auntie Lo and Uncle Jackwere, of course. Chat adored living on the West Pearl River. He loved his family of assorted characters. Maybe one day he'd travel with the Humans again, if ever there was another storm, but for him this was adventure enough. No need to go off gallivanting to find an exciting life when he already had an exciting life right here. He agreed with the big bullfrog over there.

The new Prince of Slidell would begin his training from the dock that Uncle Jackwere built this very morning. There was a special concert Ms. Whit would attend with him.

The conversation had dwindled. No one wanted to say anything, although they all knew, Ms. Whit was leaving. Jeremiah was having the hardest time of it. He wanted so much for her to stay. She had been his best teacher. They had shared more in a few days than others would in a lifetime. He knew she had stayed this long because it was so hard to say goodbye.

"So...like"....Ms. Whit's Daughter...from California, began.

"What do you..." Jeremiah said at the same time.

"Uh-oh, like you go first Jeremiah, I can wait." Ms. Whit's Daughter...from California, said.

"No, you go first, please." He said, "I can wait for the answer."

"Well, if you're fer sure, I was only going to ask my mother, like, where are you going from here?" It was out. At last, everyone could ask. They all began talking at one time.

"Yes Annabelle, m'de'ah, where will you go from he'ah?" Old Bully inquired.

Lord Chatterly added "And when will you come back?"

"Whatever will we do without you here?" asked Tutankhamen. "Who will sing for us?"

"Oh, my friends I will miss you too. You can't imagine what wonderful things I've seen and done right here on this river. There are marvels here, right under your nose. Keep your eyes open to them. Keep your ears open to the fantastic sounds all around you. For now, we are heading south. I've always wanted to know what was at the end of the river.

"Like duh, wait mother, what do you mean by 'we'? There is no 'we' in me. I thought you were, like, going on a solo adventure to discover the wonders of the universe," Ms. Whit's Daughter ...from California, said.

Just then, they all heard an odd whirring sound. Looking up into the sky, they could see the same silhouette of the same mysterious creature hovering against the dark pink light from the newly rising sun.

Who was this lovely creature who flew like a bird and was covered with fur and sparkled like moonlight on the dark surface of the West Pearl River? "Are you the HummingBunny?" The question came from a small voice underneath a leaf of an elephant ear.

Saysa Sweet Peaches nodded quickly, a huge grin spreading across her soft furry face. She hummed to the little frog hidden behind the dark colored foliage. Ms. Whit hopped over to the leaf and looked behind it for the source of the voice.

"Hello Wiggy! Come out love, come join us."

Ms. Whit placed her hand on the little frog's back and guided him to where the others were meeting the HummingBunny.

"Can Jasper come too? And Hoppy, and Dancy, and Finny too? Wiggy wanted to know.

"And Cassie and Willenor wanna meet the HummingBunny Ms. Whit. Can we all come out?" Heck asked her, the perfect look of trust and adoration on his face.

"Of course, Heck, come out everyone, come and meet the HummingBunny."

Ms. Whit didn't think she could be more surprised, but the little frogs had pulled off their secret caper very well. No one had heard a peep from them since the young ones had been sent to bed. One by one, the little frogs came out from behind the gigantic elephant ear.

"We wanted to hear everything Ms. Whit," Jasper said as he stepped into the gathering.

"Yeah, and we wanted to see it too...for ourselves," piped Hoppy Soo following Jasper.

"'Cause we been listening to That Old Mr. BullFrog telling stories ever since we hatched," explained Heck.

"Uh-hunh, and we just couldn't miss another exciting thing, not one more," Cassie said.

"And what about you Finny, did you want to hear the stories too?" Ms. Whit asked.

"Oh yes'sum! I want to hear more about the ride in the sky," said Finny.

"The ride in the sky? What ride Finny?" Ms. Whit was puzzled by the little frog's request.

"Well see, we heard the story about how you come across Jeremiah on the boat dock."

"Yeah, and then how you rose up in the sky and was flying in the middle of that old hurricane..." chimed in Heck

"But even before all that Mizz Whit, we heard how you got stuck in the whirlpool a'fore you found Jeremiah. That was excitin' to hear that story. "Ooh boy...we were all holding our breath during that tellin'." said Wiggy.

"Were you now?" Ms. Whit could not stop the grin from appearing on her face. She loved them even more. They were so sweet, so innocent, so full of wanting to learn. What would they come up with next?

"So do ya wanna hear what we did?" asked Jasper.

"What you did, Jasper?" she asked, curious what a little guy like this would come up with now.

"Yeah, me n' ever'body else made you a song. We were gonna tell all of you about it tomorrow," said Heck.

"Yeah, but we heard you say you were leavin' Flatter Rock Ms. Whit.'" said Finnian

"So please allow us to reciprocate your gifts to us, by singing for you," said Willenor.

"I think that is a marvelous idea, I am honored. But before you get started, I would like you to meet my friend, The HummingBunny" Ms. Whit sat down beside her friend.

The little group of frogs gathered around excitedly. The anticipation of seeing a creature they had no idea existed was thrilling.

"Saysa Sweet Peaches, may I introduce Jasper, Hoppy Soo, Dancy, Heck, Finny, Cassie and Willenor. They have officially joined our family and are Jeremiah's poolmates. Little ones, meet Saysa Sweet Peaches, The HummingBunny." Ms. Whit smiled broadly.

"So happy to make your acquaintance," said Willenor.

"Hello Mizz Peaches." Heck said shyly.

"Nice to meet you". Dancy did a full pirouette as she darted away.

"A pleasha' to meet you my de'ah." Finny drawled.

"How do you do?" Hoppy Soo asked, bowing extravagantly.

"Charmed!" Cassie stuck out her hand to shake Saysa's furry paw.

"Oh my guhness, you are so be-yoo-te-ful"! Jasper exclaimed.

The HummingBunny sat up straight, looked at each of the small frogs and smiled a radiant smile, humming her sonic hum. She told them each how nice it was to meet them. They were exchanging manners, niceties it's called. One should always use their manners. Even if you don't speak the same language, manners can bridge the gap to understanding someone's intentions. Manners are a reflection of your upbringing and Ms. Whit's mother told her she better not ever hear of her not using her manners. Oh, that was long ago, but my dearie it stuck. Ms. Whit simply did not have it in her to be rude or discourteous, she'd never dream of it. When Saysa finished, Ms. Whit translated, then asked them what it was they had written.

"Mother! Like, what are we, chopped sushi? Aren't you going to introduce the rest of us to your friend," Ms. Whit's daughter… from California asked, disappointed to be left out.

Ms. Whit laughed outright.

"My darling daughter, please forgive my oversight, I will indeed make your introductions." That Big Old BullFrog Travis, Lord Chatterly and Grander nodded in agreement. They all wanted to make the acquaintance of the HummingBunny.

"Saysa, may I introduce you to my darling daughter, who is visiting from California, Lizzy LulaBelle. Lizzy this is my good friend Saysa Sweet Peaches."

"She smells like the fragrance from the nest mother. Miss Sweet Peaches, it is like so c-o-o-l to finally meet you. It is such a pleasure, and I am totally delighted, really, radically."

Lizzy was practically speechless.

The Big Old BullFrog tipped his head at the furry little creature.

"It is indeed an hon'ah to make yo'ah a'quainteence my deah. Annabelle has told us so much about yo'ah ad'venchas togetha, Ah do hope you will become a reg'lar around this old Rock, it would be mighty nice to talk about differ'unt things with someone with yo'ah ex'per'e'unce."

The enormous cat rose from the rock where he had been watching the introductions. He sniffed the HummingBunny. He looked her up and down and lowered his massive head to the ground where she sat. Eye to eye, Chat looked at the funny little bird as she returned his gaze. Her eyes twinkled at him. Something unspoken passed between them. Chat knew he had made a lifelong friend. The huge cat walked over to his resting place chuckling low. He sat on the rock with a deep feeling of kinship with the strange little creature.

Jasper couldn't contain his excitement. He and the rest of the young frogs had practiced the song they wrote for Ms. Whit for two days. They even made up a dance and performed it for Boxie and his siblings.

Teodoro, Michaelito, and Giuseppe loved the number so much they volunteered to be in it if they needed them. The frogs decided they did and asked if they would be the drums. Hoppy Soo's mother Tinga showed her the way to dance a water dance and Dancy D. showed them all how to dance on the lily pads. They sat on the edge of Flatter Rock. Their smiles were large and genuine, coming from the very heart of them. They were eager to give something back to her and Ms. Whit was happy to receive.

DEB MUSSELLI 2015

Touch the Stars

She saw a star and wished that she could touch it
But soon she found that wishes have no power
To reach a star takes great Imagination
To be it - you see it – and make it who you are.
Go build the bridge
or brick by brick a stairway
That's what it takes to grab that golden ring
Take the first step, believe it, then never, never, never give in
Imagine you - Imagine me - Imagine anything
She took her dream and stepped through that open doorway
Oh, she believed and walked into the Storm
She wouldn't quit not even for an instant
And in an instant Faith and Hope were born
She built the bridge
and stone by stone a pathway
And with each step she came to understand
Believe with all your heart and soul then do it
Then you can touch the stars, oh yes you can!
(Oh yes you can).

Ms. Whit's eyes filled with emotion. She had made a difference and she knew it. She smiled at the young, new, singing sensation that called themselves Rocker, and held out her arms. They hopped to her, burying her in a cover of froglettes. They hugged and laughed for the joy they felt.

"You like it!" Jasper hopped about the rock. "You really did like it! She likes it!"

All the little frogs danced about Ms. Whit joyfully. It had been a good Coming Up. If every Coming Up was like this Coming Up then all the little frogs hoped they had a Coming Up every day or so.

"WILL-E-NOOOOR!" her mother hollered to her.

"We have to go now Ms. Whit, I heard my mother calling me," Willenor said.

"Mine too, me too, me too," the others chimed in.

"We love you Mizz Whit," Jasper yelled to her as they hopped away from the big rock.

"Wahl, I do d'clare my deah. I do believe we have us a new choir, those little 'uns put on a right lively pa'formance. I imagine they will be a sure source of entertainment," said the Big Old BullFrog.

"Jasper was always singing when we were in the waiting pools," Jeremiah told them. "He sang about anything that moved and Dancy danced to everything Jasper sang. They were a lot of fun to grow up with. I am glad we'll be seeing one another every day."

The council murmured and agreed the new singers would be a popular addition to Flatter Rock.

"Speaking of choirs, Jeremiah, I want to take you to hear something else I think you will really enjoy. Would you like to go with me?" Ms. Whit asked the new prince.

"Oh yes ma'am, it's really amazing the things that go on right under your feet!" he answered.

"Very well, the sun is almost up and it is the perfect time for you to see this. We're going to the edge of the dock Uncle Jackwere built. You'll see Jeremiah. It is an amazing concert."

Ms. Whit and the Prince of Slidell hopped off into the pink morning light for one last underwater concert for her and the first of many for Jeremiah.

"Law'd Chat, this Old Rock won't never be the same without that glorious voice," lamented the Old BullFrog.

Chat picked up his flute and started to play. He lowered the instrument and said, "You may bc right, old chap. You may be right about that indeed."

Chat played sweetly. He felt Ms. Whit's absence although she had not left the river. You could hear it in his voice when he spoke to the Old BullFrog and in the music he played

Chapter Seventeen

Don't Let Your Song Go Unsung

Jeremiah, the new Prince of Slidell, sat with Ms. Whit facing the West Pearl River. They were waiting for the sun to rise sparkling and glittering on the water. Where the light sparkled the brightest, the two frogs dove in.

Ms. Whit swam with ease to alight on the mossy root of a long dead tree stump. She motioned for Jeremiah to sit beside her and not move a muscle. The mussels were going to sing. She knew they would. They always did.

The entire underwater community slept, swaying in the current of the cool water until the music awakened them. Slowly and softly, it began. The gentle ripple of sound spread through the river. The blue gill woke. The crawfish stirred. The grasses swayed and Ms. Whit rose to the sounds of the melody. Jeremiah watched her underwater dance. He couldn't believe this happened every morning.

What else was happening as he slept or played amongst the lily pads? What other glorious thing was he missing? Did the clouds march to the sound of the wind? Perhaps they did. He could not know. He had never been there. Did flowers sing? He had never listened. What were the beetles and bugs talking about? How many times had Saysa Sweet Peaches passed over Flatter Rock and no one knew? What other creatures were there? Were there any others?

Oh, what glorious sounds. Ms. Whit told him all there was to tell about the Songs of the Mussels. Telling could not come close to being there. She was right; it was not something that could be easily described.

This was magical. He knew he would come here often. He knew he would share with the others as long as the mussels would let him come.

The sounds began to take shape. It was music. It was themed. It had rhythm. It had a form you felt you could reach out and touch, but instead, it touched you. The music was a palpable thing.

Ms. Whit motioned to Jeremiah. It was time to surface. Oh, too soon, too soon! The music slowed. It echoed off the stones on the bottom of the river. It drifted down the river, softened then became subdued.

They swam to the surface of the water. Ms. Whit hopped upon the lily pad, Jeremiah at her side. The soft whirring sound of wings hovered above the lily pad. Saysa Sweet Peaches landed beside them, her wings folding gently behind her.

"Good morning, your majesty, it is good to see you this fine morning." She curtsied to the new Prince. The others will be ready soon. The journey begins at the tip of the tallest pine tree. We will gather there," hummed the bunny.

"I will be there. I'll take Prince Jeremiah back to Flatter Rock and say my goodbyes," she replied.

Saysa Sweet Peaches zipped away to join the large flock of HummingBunnies gathering for the flight south. The two frogs hopped towards the large flat rock.

Jeremiah stopped halfway there. The small white frog stopped beside him in the pathway.

selli 2015
BRISTLING
Deb Musselli 2015

Jeremiah said to her, “Ms. Whit, I…I gotta thank you. I know why you are leaving. If all these wonders can be in our own backyard then there is no limit to what there is to see in the world.” Jeremiah smiled at her.

“Jeremiah, my sweet little prince, you have a song to sing. It is a fabulous song. Yours alone. Everyone has their very own song. Just waiting to be heard. Don’t let yours go unsung, your life unlived. Use your imagination, fly! You can. See it crystal clear like the Salamander’s stream, then do it. Do it then lead others in your choir. After all, you are the prince. Believe. Believe it into being.”

They followed the trail back to Flatter Rock. When they reached the grassy riverbank, Ms. Whit saw all the frogs she had spent the past few years with. Her friends. Her family. Chat rested on Tutankhamen’s back. The dragonflies danced above their heads, darting, flitting, landing on Chat’s ear. He twitched it away. Life went on, just exactly as it always does.

It would go on for her too, but there would be a difference. Now she knew. This was the way it was supposed to happen for her. She believed she could do it and so she did it. It wasn’t an accident. There were no bolts of lightning, no celebrations, no appointment needed. Ms. Whit could fly. All she had to do was use her imagination.

“Listen up everybody! Come to the Rock! Come in close all you sweet baby frogs, the old, the new, the green, the blue. Fish and Fowl! Crawl or walk come one and all. It is time to say good-bye! They all came, walking, hopping, flying, crawling or swimming. They all wanted to say good-bye.

It seemed as if everything frogs do was a huge production. I’ve seen the little frogs gathered on the banks of the river and stock tanks and ponds. This has got to be what they are doing, having a Coming Up. Well, after a little while had passed, I’m not sure how long since frogs don’t have watches or clocks, but after a little while, they gathered to give Ms. Whit the sendoff they thought she deserved. Big and flashy and full of music. They sang all her favorite songs and a few she had not yet heard.

Suddenly, a flash of an iridescent feather from a fast-moving wing appeared above Ms. Whit.

“Shall we fly?” Saysa Sweet Peaches hummed.

“I’m ready! Good-bye West Pearl River! I will always love you!”

And just like that, Ms. Whit disappeared.

The End

About the Author

Born in San Antonio Texas, Debbie Woodward Musselli now lives in Leander Texas with her sister Kay. Debbie professes to be an extraordinary doodler. Having enjoyed the art since she was a very young child. She has been a poet since third grade, often helping other kids in her class with poetry assignments. Debbie now writes poetry and stories for children along with illustrating these writings.
Her other publications are amongst a compilation of artists and writers who came together to publish " Come To The Gathering" and illustrating "Max's Magically Imaginary Forest" written by 6 year old Max Riojas, Debbie's grandson.

Ms. Whit is Debbie's latest explosion into imagining what one can do with a small backyard and a limitless desire to "just believe."

Special Thanks

Special thanks to Barbara Hunley for photography, Yash Sharma and Matthew Coleman for graphic design, Sara Henry for her love and support, , and to my beloved Aunt Sara, truly the real Ms. Whit.

In loving memory of Joseph M. Musselli, thank you for Dolly.

Dictionary

A

Absence – the state of being away from a place or person.

Absentmindedly – having or showing a habitually forgetful or inattentive disposition

Accidental – happening by chance, unintentionally, or unexpectedly.

Accustomed – customary; usual.

Acquaintance – a person one knows slightly, but who is not a close friend.

Adoration – deep love and respect.

Albeit – although.

Amazed – greatly surprised; astonished.

Ancient – of or pertaining to a remote period.

Approach – come near to someone.

Arias – a long accompanied song for a solo voice.

Articles – a particular item or object.

Assigned – allocate a job or duty.

Assortment – a miscellaneous collection of things or people.

Auspicious – conducive to success; favorable.

B

Bated breath – to take away one's breath.

Blushed – show shyness, embarrassment, or shame by becoming red in the face.

Boardwalk – a wooden walkway across sand or marshy ground.

Bounding – walk or run with leaping strides.

Braving the storm – endure or face without showing fear.

Brilliantly – in a very bright or dazzling way.

C

Caper – skip or dance about in a lively or playful way.

Casting – shedding light on something.

Chameleon – a small slow-moving lizard with eyes that rotate independently; with a highly developed ability to change colors.

Cheesecloth – thin, loosely woven cloth of cotton.

Chuckled – laugh quietly or inwardly.

Clenched – of the fingers or hand closed tight ball.

Clever – quick to understand, learn, or apply ideas; intelligent.

Cocoon – envelop or surround in a protective or comforting way.

Communicate – share or exchange information, news, or ideas.

Communication – the imparting or exchanging of information or news.

Competing – striving against one another to gain or win something.

Composure – the state or feeling of being calm and in control of oneself.
Cooperate – work jointly toward the same end.
Complemented - add to in a way that enhances or improves it.
Congregation – a gathering or collection of people, animals, or things.
Companion – a person or animal with whom one spends a lot of time or with whom one travels.
Coronation – the ceremony of crowning a sovereign or a sovereign's consort.
Coincidence – a remarkable concurrence of events or circumstances without apparent causal connection.
Consequences – a result or effect of an action or condition.
Committee – a group of people appointed for a specific function, typically consisting of members of a larger group.
Compensate – give someone something in recognition of loss.
Council – an advisory, deliberative, or legislative body of people formally constituted and meeting regularly.
Croaked – of a frog or crow; make a characteristic deep hoarse sound.

D

Dabbed – press against (something) lightly with a piece of absorbent material in order to clean or dry it.
Daydreaming – indulge in daydreams.
Dazzled – of a bright light, blinded temporarily.
Debris – scattered pieces of waste or remains.
Déjà vu – a feeling of having already experienced the present situation.
Delivered – bring and hand over to the proper recipient or address.
Desperately – in a way that shows despair.
Destiny – the events that will necessarily happen to a particular person or thing in the future.
Determined – having made a firm decision and being resolved not to change it.
Dire – extremely serious or urgent.
Discovered – find something unexpectedly or in the course of a search.
Diverted – cause someone or something to change course or turn from one direction to another.
Documented – record something in written, photographic, or other form.
Drenched – wet thoroughly, soak.
Dumbfounded – greatly astonished or amazed.

E

Embarrassment – a feeling of self-consciousness, shame, or awkwardness.
Enigma – a person or thing that is mysterious, puzzling.
Energy – the strength and vitality required for sustained physical or mental activity.
Enormous – very large in size, quantity, or extent.
Enormously – to a very great degree or extent; considerably.
Epic – narrating the deeds and adventures of heroic or legendary figures or the history of a nation.
Erratically – unpredictable manner or pattern
Entryway – a way in to somewhere or something; an entrance.

Envy – a feeling of discontentment or resentful longing aroused by someone else's possessions, qualities, or luck.
Expense – the cost required for something; the money spent on something.

F

Faraway – distant in space or time.
Flip -flopping - Move with a flapping motion.
Ferocious – savagely fierce, cruel, or violent.
Festive – relating to a festival.
Flitting – move swiftly and lightly.
Focal point – relating to the center or main point of interest.
Foreign – strange and unfamiliar.
Fragrance – a pleasant, sweet smell.
Free-fall – downward movement under the force of gravity only.
Frustrated – feeling distress and annoyance, especially because of inability to change something.

G

Gadgets – a small device or tool, especially an ingenious or novel one.
Gasped – inhale suddenly with the mouth open, out of pain or astonishment.
Genuine – truly what something is said to be; authentic.
Gleaming – reflecting light.
Glided – move with a smooth continuous motion, typically with little noise.
Gooey – soft and sticky.
Gruyere cheese – a firm, tangy cheese.

H

HummingBunny – Imaginary creature. Part hummingbird and part rabbit.
Hurled – throw an object with great force.

I

Imagination – the action of forming ideas not present to the senses
Imagining – form a mental image or concept of
Immediately – at once, instantly.
Intricate – very complicated or detailed
Intently – with earnest and eager attention
Intentions – a thing intended, an aim or plan.
Inspector – an official employed to ensure that official regulations are obeyed.
Iridescent – showing luminous colors that seem to change when seen from different angles.

J

Joyfully – with great pleasure and happiness

K

Keen – highly developed.
Kerfuffle – a commotion or fuss.

L

Lamented – a conventional way of describing something that has been lost or that has ceased to exist.
Lullaby – a quiet, gentle song sung to send a child to sleep.

M

Magnificent – impressively beautiful, elaborate, or extravagant; striking.
Marmalade – a sweet food made from citrus fruit and sugar boiled to a thick consistency.
Marvelous – causing great wonder; extraordinary.
Melody – a sequence of single notes that is musically satisfying.
Mesmerized – hold the attention of someone to the exclusion of all else or so as to transfix them.
Meticulously – in a way that shows great attention to detail.
Mid-air – a part or section of the air above ground level or above another surface.
Miniature – a much smaller size than normal; very small.
Mission – a strongly felt aim, ambition, or calling.
Miscalculated – calculate an amount, distance, or measurement wrongly.
Miscellaneous – of various types or from different sources.
Motionless – not moving; stationary.
Mumbled – say something indistinctly and quietly, making it difficult for others to hear.
Murmured – say something in a low, soft, or indistinct voice.

N

Nectar – a sugary liquid secreted especially by flowers.
Nosedive – a steep downward plunge by an aircraft. Or a frog plunging into a bowl of cut up okra pods.
Notion – a conception of or belief about something.

O

Occurrence – an incident or event.
Official – relating to an authority or public body and its duties, actions, and responsibilities.
Operatic – relating to or characteristic of opera.
Organized – arranged in a systematic way.
Outlay – the act of expending.

P

Papier-mache' – a malleable mixture consisting of paper pieces or pulp, sometimes reinforced with textiles, bound with an adhesive, such as glue, starch, or wallpaper paste that becomes hard.

Parish – a local church community composed of the members of a Protestant church.

Partially – only in part; to a limited extent.

Passel – a large group of people or things of indeterminate number; a pack.

Passion – strong and barely controllable emotion.

Peering – (peer) look keenly or with difficulty at someone or something.

Perch – a thing on which a bird or other entity alights or roosts.

Perspective – the art of drawing solid objects on a two-dimensional surface so as to give the right impression of their height, width, depth, and position in relation to each other when viewed from a particular point.

Pirouette – an act of spinning on one foot, typically with the raised foot touching the knee of the supporting leg.

Pollen – a fine powdery substance from the male part of a flower.

Ponder – think about something carefully.

Practicing – perform a skill repeatedly in order to improve proficiency.

Practically – virtually; almost.

Predicament – a difficult, unpleasant, or embarrassing situation.

Predictable – able to be predicted.

Precariously – in a way that is not securely in position and is likely to fall or collapse.

Promptly – with little or no delay; immediately.

Q

Quicksilver – the liquid metal mercury. Also, a super-fast character in the X-men movies.

R

Racket – a loud unpleasant noise; a din.

Reassuringly – in a way that removes someone's doubts and fears.

Reciprocate – respond to a gesture or action by making a corresponding one.

Rehearsed – practice a play, piece of music, or other work for later public performance.

Retrieved – get or bring back; regain possession of.

Reunion – an instance of two or more people coming together again after a period of separation.

Rhythm – a strong, regular, repeated pattern of movement or sound.

Rumble – make a continuous deep, resonant sound.

Rummaging – search unsystematically and untidily through a mass or receptacle.

S

Scampered – run with quick light steps, especially through fear or excitement.

Scant – barely sufficient or adequate.

Scooped – pick up and move something with a scoop.

Shambles – a state of total disorder.
Sheepishly – in a manner due to a lack of self confidence.
Skimmed – go or move quickly and lightly over or on a surface or through the air.
Snatched – quickly seize in a rude or eager way.
Sonic – denoting relating to, or of the nature of sound or sound waves.
Spasm – a sudden involuntary muscular contraction or convulsive movement.
Spectacular – beautiful in a dramatic and eye-catching way.
Speechless – unable to speak, especially as the temporary result of shock or some strong emotion.
Splendidly – in a magnificent or very impressive manner.
Squashed – crush or squeeze something with force so that it becomes flat, soft, or out of shape.
Streamlined – having a form that presents very little resistance to the flow of air or water.
Stricken – seriously affected by an undesirable condition or unpleasant feeling.
Sufficiently – to an adequate degree; enough or difficult to understand.
Survey – to examine as to condition, situation, or value.
Swayed – move or cause to move slowly or rhythmically backward and forward or from side to side.

T

Temptation – the desire to do something, especially something wrong or unwise.
Tendril – a threadlike appendage of a climbing plant growing in a spiral form.
Thunderous – relating to or giving warning of thunder.
Tousled – untidy.
Translated – express the sense of words in another language.
Trembling – shaking or quivering, typically as a result of anxiety, excitement, or frailty.
Triangular – shaped like a triangle; having three sides and three corners.
Triumph – a great victory or achievement.
Trot – to proceed or cause to proceed at a pace faster than a walk.
Troupe – a group of dancers, actors, or other entertainers who tour to different venues.

U

Umpteenth – used to emphasize that something has happened on many occasions.
Unaware – having no knowledge of a situation or fact.
Unbeatable – not able to be defeated as in a contest.
Uncommon – out of the ordinary.
Undignified – appearing foolish and unseemly, lacking in dignity.
Unique – being the only one of its kind; unlike anything else.
Unusual – not commonly occurring or done.
Uprooted – pull something, especially a tree or plant out of the ground.
Utterly – completely and without qualification; absolutely.

V

Various – more than one; several.

Vegetarian – a person who does not eat meat.

Venture – a risky or daring journey or undertaking.

Vibration – an instance of vibrating

Victorious – having won a victory; triumphant.

Vivid – producing powerful feelings or strong, clear images in the mind.

W

Waddle – walk with short steps and a clumsy swaying motion.

Whirlpool – a rapidly rotating mass of water in a river or sea into which objects may be drawn.

Witnessed – to see something take place.

Whoosh – move or cause to move quickly or suddenly with a rushing sound.

Woodwork – the wooden parts of a room or building such as windows frames or doors.

Wreckage – the remains of something that has been badly damaged or destroyed.

Wrestled – struggle with a difficulty or problem.

Wretched – in a very unhappy or unfortunate state.

X

Xanadu – an idyllic, exotic, or luxurious place.

Y

Yielding – giving way under pressure, not hard or rigid.

Yodeled – practice a form of singing or calling marked by rapid alternation between the normal voice and falsetto.

Z

Zagazig – city in northern Egypt north northeast of Cairo.

Note to parents: I put this dictionary together for kids and parents. The definitions are from the dictionary included in Word or directly from Merriam-Webster. If there is more than one definition, I used the one that fits the situation. I hope it comes in handy.

Glossary

Auntie Kay-Kay – Sister to the author. Also known as Auntie Kay-Kay.

Auntie Lo – Human living with Uncle Jackwere. Married for 56 years. Auntie to Auntie Kay-Kay.

Auntie Polly Woggles – That Big Old BullFrog Travis' mother.

Auntie Toadie McRoadie – Scottish Frog from Auchenshoogle. Lives in a cracked clay pot on the East bank of The West Pearl River. Came to "Down Below" from a transport ship heading to New York City.

Axolotl - Mexican salamander. Able to dance and yodel. Found also in one particularly cold mountain stream in the Northwestern United States. Specifically, Colorado.

BackPipe – Large white polyvinyl chloride, pvc drain pipe extending about nine inches above ground in The Great Backyard. Pipe runs underground and winds up at the bottom of the West Pearl River and opens into the water. Original intended use unknown. When the Wind blows over the pipe at just the exact angle it sounds like a bagpipe playing.

Baton Rouge – State capital of Louisiana. Birthplace of AnnaBelle Whit.

Beloved Piano Stool - Housing for Ms. Whit.

Boxie Tortusie – Italian Box Turtle. Extremely pleasant disposition.

Coming Up – Celebration of any upcoming event involving dancing, dining, singing, games and music.

Cowboy Opera - Songs Grander sings written to the tune of famous operatic arias. Words have been changed to suit the Cowboys on the ranch and so the chickens will lay better eggs.

Daphne – Mr. Hawthorne's huge, I mean very big, Old English Mastiff dog. Daphne weighs in at just under 173 pounds. She is a beautiful dog and loves children and spinning Turtles.

Debra – Imaginary Hurricane.

Dolly – Dragonfly with a short memory span.

Down Below – Area down below Flatter Rock.

Escargot – Snails….able to dance.

Flatter Rock – Large red stone overhanging the banks of the West Pearl River. Gathering place for all sorts of creatures and events.

Froglettes – All girl singing group.

Grander – Ms. Whit's grandfather. Cowboy from Choke Canyon, Texas. Sings Cowboy opera. Rides on a horned toad named Thistle-Lee.

The Great Backyard – The backyard at Auntie Lo and Uncle Jackwere's. It has so many great things to see and do that whenever visitors come they tell Auntie Lo and Uncle Jackwere what a great backyard they have so the title stuck and became a proper name.

The Great Back Porch – Same thing happened to the back porch.

The Great House – Ditto the house. It is a virtual museum of neat and wonderful artifacts. Art, comfortable furniture and delightful collectibles.

Great Father MistleToad – also known as Great Father MistleToady. Founder of Flatter Rock. Father to That Big Old BullFrog Travis' great, great, great, grandmother.

Human beings – Humans to the animal world.

HummingBunny – Rare species of animal bird mix. Uses extreme speed in flight. Creates an odd whirring sound when flying. Creatures are a combination of bird and rabbit. Found across the United States though mainly in Texas and Louisiana. There is a great rack of HummingBunnies in Colorado.

HummingBunny Nest – Made of cattail down and tender grapevines. Home to Saysa Sweet Peaches and other HummingBunnies.

In-a-gada-da-vida – No association whatsoever. Needed an 'I' word.

Lord Chatterly – Largest Maine Coon striped cat in Louisiana. Very well educated. Flutist. Companion to Tutankhamun. Best furry feline friend to Ms. Whit.

Mildred Millipede – Xylophonist.

Mussels – Underwater crustaceans with the ability to sing and make extraordinary music underwater. Extremely shy. Introverted except when singing.

Mortimer McGillicuddy – Retired Inspector of the search for the next Prince of Slidell.

Ms. Whit – Small white Frog who learns to use her imagination. Singing Frog. Mother to Lizzy LulaBelle. Flies across the country using her imagination. Re:The author's imagination.

Ms. Whit's Daughter...from California, - Resident Valley Girl. Loves to travel. Spells words to be clever. Given name Lizzy LulaBelle.

Queen of Hearts – In another story written by a different author.

Robin – Auntie Lo's favorite house cat.

Saysa Sweet Peaches – HummingBunny. Extraordinarily fast flyer. Rare. Friendly disposition. Best friend to Ms Whit. Confidant. Hums to communicate. Races the Wind. Lives in the top of a tall pine tree in a nest made of cattail down and tender grapevines. Smells like Honeysuckle. Gregarious nature.

Thistle-Lee – Horny Toad. Grander's palomino. Greatest ride a Cowboy Frog could ever hope for.

Travis – County in Texas.

Tutankhamun – Resident all around friend to the community. Loves to sun on Flatter Rock with Lord Chatterly. Does not care for Daphne turning him upside down and spinning him until his eyes cross.

Uncle Jackwere - Human living with Auntie Lo. Married for 56 years.

Underwater Songs – Songs the Mussels sing that cannot be described by you or me.

Valentine's Blues – Song written by Debbie Musselli about Valentine's Day from a nine year old boy's perspective. Great when sung to the tune of the macaroni and cheese blues song. Has nothing to do with The Prince of Slidell but like the letter Q, I needed a fill in.

The West Pearl River – The river that runs through the parish where Auntie Lo and Uncle Jackwere live.

Xylophone – Musical instrument played by Mildred Millipede.

Yes – The first word Ms Whit said when she learned to use her Imagination.

Zardiack, Prince – Former Prince of Slidell. Taken by a band of ruthless bandits. Whereabouts unknown.

Coloring Pages

Robin

www.ingramcontent.com/pod-product-compliance
Lightning Source LLC
LaVergne TN
LVHW060504170826
845677LV00026B/1558

* 9 7 9 8 9 8 8 7 2 7 4 7 7 *